Entering the Civil Aircraft Industry

Business Realities at the Technological Frontier

Dean C Roberts PhD

First published by Dog Ear Publishing
4011 Vincennes Rd
Indianapolis, IN 46268
www.dogearpublishing.net

ISBN: 978-1-4575-5241-0

This book is printed on acid-free paper.

Printed in the United States of America

To my mother, Joy,

and

my two daughters, Megan and Elinor

Contents

Preface

My passion for the civil aircraft industry business started in March 1996. My manager had sent me to a factory in the middle of the Brazilian hinterland, which was really quite a strange experience for me. My employer, Rolls-Royce, had recently bought an aircraft engine company, Allison Engine Company in Indianapolis, which, apart from having strong positions in various defense platforms, had launched a new engine program that was going to power two new civil aircraft. The engine was being applied to a turboprop-powered aircraft called the Saab 2000. More intriguingly, though, a version of the engine was going to power an aircraft called the EMB 145, later to be called the ERJ 145. This aircraft was produced by a Brazilian company called Embraer.

At the time, Embraer was a little-known company in the aircraft industry and our engine was going to be used on the new civil airliner, the EMB 145, that this Brazilian company was bringing to the marketplace. Rolls-Royce management had to have a view on whether this aircraft program was going to be successful and whether Embraer itself was going to survive. So my manager, who was the head of Rolls-Royce's strategic planning department, asked me to visit Embraer with a colleague to try to understand the nature of the company and tasked us to come back with a view on whether the company and the ERJ 145 had a long-term future.

At the time, the prospects were not good for Embraer. In the prior year, 1995, the company had had sales of $295 million but, disastrously, had had losses of $258 million. This was remarkable, eye-wateringly poor financial performance, and previous years had not been much better.

I must admit, I was rather skeptical about the company's chances. After having spoken to the people at Embraer and having looked at some of their plans and their strong, impressive order book for the ERJ 145, however, I was intrigued. On my return to the UK after much further analysis and financial modeling of the prospects of the company, it was concluded that this organization potentially did have a chance.

Of course, the rest is history, as those who are well aware of the civil aircraft industry know. Embraer is now the third-largest civil aircraft manufacturer in the world, behind Boeing and Airbus. In 2014, it had sales of $6.3 billion and had an order book of $23 billion.

When I was at the company in the mid-1990s, such a prospect did not look feasible. It is remarkable that it has succeeded, given the track record of so many failures of attempted entry into the civil aircraft industry. I was really fascinated by this as my career developed.

After seven years in company headquarters' strategic planning at Derby, England, in 1999, I moved to Allison Engine Company—it is now called Rolls-Royce Corporation—in Indianapolis and was involved in strategy aspects and looking at the future.

When Rolls-Royce acquired Allison, the products made there were smaller engines, not engines for the big airliners that many readers will be familiar with from Airbus and Boeing. The facility made engines for business jets, helicopters, military transports, and a new phenomenon at the time—regional jets. At that time there were a lot of new entrants into the civil aircraft market and we were putting plans together with the aim of hanging our engines on their aircraft. I was privy to the details of these programs and had to make judgments on the market prospects for these proposed aircraft.

Over the years, I have looked at Indonesia, Korea, India, Japan, Russia, and other countries in terms of their aspirant civil aircraft programs and whether they are going to be successful. This book taps into that experience and tries to make some sense of what makes an entrant into the civil aircraft industry successful.

There is a gap in the books about entry barriers to the civil aircraft industry, though numerous books and academic papers exist about specific airline industry campaigns and aircraft programs. One that comes to mind is the quintessential *The Sporty Game* by John Newhouse, which is a fantastic exposé of the inside story of the early days of the wide-body civil aircraft campaigns. Other books that come to mind include autobiographies by esteemed engineers or businesspeople, such as *Not Much of an Engineer"* by Stanley Hooker, the famous Rolls-Royce engineer who was involved in the early stages of the Rolls-Royce RB211 engine. There are also many books out there about specific countries' aircraft programs; a good example is the excellent book *China Airborne*, by James Fallows. Until now, however, there has not been a review, a book, or an analysis that looks at the industry as a whole, examining what makes entry difficult and what things make entry more likely for an aspirant civil aircraft manufacturer. This book addresses that gap.

The scale of the civil aircraft industry is massive. A typical research-and-development program for a civil aircraft starts at $700 million and can easily go up to $10 billion for an aircraft like the Airbus A380, so entry barriers in an absolute financial sense are high. The other challenges of this industry, however, are technological, commercial, and, in some cases, geopolitical. These will all be addressed in this book.

The introduction chapter will provide you more details about the structure of the book, but I want to reiterate my view that this industry is fascinating and worthy of study. It involves ambitious companies and determined governments. The reality of governmental power and intervention really struck me as I did my research. This book tries to bring out the reality about technological development, which is less about invention and more about innovation. It explores how a high-technology industry develops and how companies strive to compete at the technological barrier. I hope you become as fascinated by the industry as I am.

Dean C. Roberts,
Leesburg, Virginia
September 2016

Acknowledgments

A special thank-you goes to my friend, colleague, and mentor, Jim Burroughs at the McIntire School of Commerce at the University of Virginia, who guided me into the world of academia and continues to be a great sounding board. My thanks also go to Carl Zeithaml, Rick Netemeyer, and David Lehman for taking the risk and letting me loose on their students. Similarly, I wish to thank Bernard Carlson, Eric Loth, and Xiaodong (Chris) Li, from the School of Engineering and Applied Science. Through my interactions and questioning with students from Commerce and Engineering, I will always continue to learn.

I also gratefully acknowledge the support of my employer, Rolls-Royce, for allowing me to progress with this book. Special thanks go to those individuals who provided advice to me over my many years at the company, including Charles Coltman, Simon Hart, David Hygate, Richard Campbell, Tom Hartmann, Ian Aitken, Scott Shannon, Steve Friedrich, Rafael Andrino, Alan Stiley, Tom Dale, Will Powers, Mike Elliott, Lorin Sodell, Jeff Merrell, John Whurr and Peter J Johnston.

At this stage, I want to mention two individuals who have been very important in my formative thinking on this book. One is Simon Hart, who was my boss in charge of Rolls-Royce strategic planning. He took me on as a raw market analyst, and I would like to think that after the seven years I worked with him, I came out of his department as a fairly knowledgeable, good advisor on the realities of doing business at the technological frontier. I was exposed to strategy in its grandest sense, which included the concept of business entry barriers and organizational behavior. In addition, I also developed in my understanding of financial models, why people make the decisions they do, the realities of government intervention and developed a skill to observe what companies actually do rather than accepting what they say they will do. That whole experience came as a profound education to me when I was working in Simon's department. I am eternally grateful to Simon for pointing me in the right direction and for being a great mentor to me during the time I worked for him.

Simon has an interesting British sense of humor, and the notion of sending me to some place in the middle of the Brazilian forest to visit Embraer was quite amusing to him. He later sent me on a strategy development job to Winnipeg in Canada in the middle of the winter, for which, being a rather naïve individual at the time, I didn't pack appropriate clothing. This caused him much amusement, and we have often joked about it when I have met up with him over the years.

The other person I would like to mention as a major influence on me is Professor Riti Singh of Cranfield University. He was my PhD supervisor at Cranfield when I was working on my thesis. After several years of being in strategic planning, I wanted to look at the subject of entry barriers in a more academic, rigorous sense, and Rolls-Royce was kind enough to support me in carrying out a research-based PhD.

I look back on the conversations I had over the years with Riti and realize that every one of them was an enlightening, with profound insight. Those conversations kept me going for many months in exploring some of the aspects of industry entry barriers and the realities of complex product systems. I still seek Riti's counsel on issues, and he is very gracious in his advice. It is a pleasure working with him. I see this book as part of the pleasure of "giving back" that he instilled in me during our many conversations.

Other people who have provided insight, advice and counsel over the years include Rollie Vincent, Glynis Priester, Alex Youngs, Ann Battle Macheras, John Stack, and João Paiva. In particular, I am indebted to Peder Andersen, now an independent consultant but once the aerospace industry expert at the US International Trade Commission. I enjoy our conversations on the industry and appreciate him being a sounding board for some of the ideas expressed in this book.

Extra special thanks go to three strong women. First is my mother, Joy, who has been a constant source of inspiration for me. I volunteered her to read through the early drafts of this book. She took on this task with great enthusiasm, and her feedback was much appreciated. I also want to mention my two daughters, Megan and Elinor. In their own way, they have both inspired me with their resilience and dedication to their vision even through tough times. All three are amazing ladies.

Finally, the usual caveat: All responsibility for errors or omissions in this book lies with me. Opinions expressed are my own and are not necessarily endorsed by either the University of Virginia or Rolls-Royce.

1.

Introduction

This book is an accessible guide to one of the world's most fascinating industries, civil aircraft manufacturing. The industry is fascinating because it has so many facets. These facets make its study an excellent way to learn about globalized industries operating at the technological frontier.

The book is designed to be easily read in three or four sessions, so it is short by design. Why short? The intent is for it to be read! Realistically and pragmatically, thick books tend not to be read. That is the track record. Because this subject area is fascinating, I have tried hard to make the book as readable as possible. I am keen to introduce the industry to others, so I hope it will be read from cover to cover.

Civil aircraft are extremely complex machines. One of the challenges for a new entrant to the industry is that they will have to operate at the technological barrier to be competitive with the incumbents. Another challenge is in managing the large level of capital investment, establishing sophisticated production facilities, creating supply chains, and deploying a global service support network. Further challenges are presented by geopolitical aspects of and pervasive role of government intervention in the industry.

Most countries aspire to have a civil aircraft industry. They see having such an industry as the next step up the value chain of products. What they fail to realize is that this transition is not easy to navigate. There are step changes between undertaking low-level manufacturing tasks and putting together an aircraft that will be certifiable for use by fare-paying passengers.

This book is aimed at businesspeople with an interest in aerospace but also generally interested in high technology and business strategy. There are many lessons to be learned from looking at various aspects of the civil aircraft manufacturing industry. To illustrate this, the book will touch on many case studies as we explore the business and its complexity and dynamics.

In addition to businesspeople, the book is aimed squarely toward business and engineering students, as I am an engineer and a businessperson. Often, the communities of business and engineering find it hard to interact and to communicate. Here, I aim to expand each specialist's worldview by looking at civil aircraft from both engineering and business perspectives, blending the two aspects into one view of the industry.

Much can be learned from the civil aircraft industry and applied to other high-technology sectors. The civil aircraft industry operates at the technological leading edge and has high government involvement. If you can understand aspects of civil aircraft manufacturing, you can therefore examine many other industries with the same set of tools and analytical frameworks.

Another potential audience for this book is people engaged in government policy. Admittedly, this book is not meant to be a deep treatise on industrial policy, and there are many works available from various sources on industrial policy, but this book addresses the issue from a practitioner's point of view. The idea is to try to take lessons from the industry's successes and failures and draw conclusions for other real-world situations.

The final audience I have in mind is academics. The idea of this book is to stimulate academia's interest in the civil aircraft sector as a way to teach globalization and the development of company strategy. Throughout the book, I provide many references to useful publications, journal articles, and folios that can be helpful in further research about the subject.

At this stage, it is probably worthwhile to define what I mean by civil aircraft manufacturing. Certainly, we are looking at familiar companies like Boeing and Airbus that produce large airliners sold to the world's airlines. These two companies are incumbents. We will be also looking at Embraer of Brazil and Bombardier of Canada, who make regional aircraft. They are also incumbents. In addition, we will be considering aspirant companies from countries such as Russia, Japan, and China and examine the chances of their success or failure.

In scope, we will be covering very specifically the civil jet aircraft business, including fifty seater regional aircraft and larger. This includes, for example, Bombardier CRJ regional jets, the Airbus A320 family, and the Boeing 777. It does not include turboprop-powered aircraft, business jets, or very small aircraft that readers may observe at their local airports. These latter sectors have separate and different industrial dynamics, and each is worthy of a book in its own right.

This book is about civil jet aircraft industry entry, but this needs to be defined yet further. Industry entry has to be on a global scale and long term, so delivery of an aircraft solely to the manufacturer's domestic customer base does not meet this definition. Neither does the situation in which a manufacturer produces just one aircraft type and does not develop a follow-on product. The threshold defined here is therefore high, and only four industries have achieved entry: the US, Europe, Canada, and Brazil.

Although we will be considering principally the civil aircraft sector, the other area we will explore, where appropriate, is the civil aircraft engine scene, as there are lessons to be learned from this sector that will illuminate the civil aircraft scene. This is because engine companies operate in a parallel dynamic of government involvement, technological challenge, and large-scale investment.

The contents of the book will start, as one would expect, with some foundational concepts that address economic fundamentals. The reader requires grounding in some basic economics subjects as comparative advantage and the theories of entry barriers into industries. Those will be addressed with a light touch from a practitioner's perspective in Chapter 2.

Similarly, in Chapter 3, we will look at some of the theoretical aspects of innovation, innovation compared to invention, and the various industrial policy approaches deployed by governments.

Chapter 4 will address high-technology products and will introduce the notion of complex product systems. Civil aircraft are part of this latter grouping of products. A complex product is a hugely complex machine. It is different from the products that most people interact with in their day-to-day lives, such as cell phones and computers. Complex products are usually sold in low volumes and are characterized by a high level of technology embodiment and interrelatedness of the various components of the product. Chapter 4 will explain the important subject of complex products, which unfortunately is little researched in the literature but is actually an important part of most developed nations' manufacturing bases.

Readers who feel that they do not need the theoretical aspects may skip foundational chapters 2 and 3, and perhaps even 4, jumping straight into the book at Chapter 5 if their only interest is the specifics of the civil aircraft industry and if they feel they do not need the theoretical aspects.

Chapter 5 will provide an introduction to the basics of the civil aircraft industry. We will review the business model, the various participants of the aircraft industry, and, again, the complexity of civil aircraft. In this chapter, we will start getting closer to discussing the civil aircraft industry itself, rather than the prior chapters, which are more foundational.

Chapter 6 provides a more detailed explanation and exploration of the barriers to entry in the civil aircraft industry. Although the subject is introduced in the foundational chapters of the book, Chapter 6 is much more specific about the civil aircraft industry.

An important exploration of the role of government in civil aircraft manufacturing is included in Chapter 7. The gamut of funding mechanisms and their rationales will be discussed, including capital market failure, industry targeting, and strategic trade theory. Their consideration will set up the analytical framework for thinking about this industry later in the book. Also in Chapter 7 are reviews of several countries and regions, covering why and how they support their civil aircraft industries. The US support mechanism is very different from the European experience, as the Brazilian approach is very different from, say, the Japanese scene.

Chapter 8 considers some additional thoughts on entry barriers. Whereas much of the framework in the earlier chapters is based on largely theoretical ideas about what constitute entry barriers, Chapter 8 introduces some practical real-world entry barriers that are very pertinent for civil aircraft manufacturing. This includes, for example, the consideration of how a country defends itself. For instance, if a US-provided defense umbrella is over an allied nation, this has implications for the domestic defense industry of that nation. This has a knock-on effect on the domestic civil aircraft industry.

The other aspect we will be discussing in Chapter 8 is the relationships between partnering strategies of new entrants with incumbents and exploring the balance of power between those two entities. We will be considering whether becoming a partner with an incumbent is a worthwhile entry route. It is not as straightforward as one might first anticipate. Chapter 8 explores this fascinating conundrum that such an arrangement can produce.

Chapter 9 performs a review of the incumbents' civil aircraft industries and how they entered the sector. We will look at the US, Europe, Brazil and Canada's industries. We look at how each country/region entered the sector, without going into a deep historical analysis. This analysis is then used to draw lessons later in the book.

In Chapter 10, I comment on the aspiring nations—Russia, China, and Japan: How are they attempting industry entry? What is the governmental engagement for these nations?

Then, in Chapter 11, I will develop a framework for assessing whether a particular entry strategy is going to be successful. This framework will be based on the foregoing chapters and will look at what has worked and what has failed in the past. Here, I will bring in all the descriptive elements from Chapters 2 through to Chapter 10 and collect the concepts into a coherent framework. This framework can then be deployed to examine other nations with aspirations to enter into the civil aircraft industry and will help us make judgments on whether they will be successful.

Finally, in Chapter 12, we will review the themes of the book and consider the implications. I will consider other aspirant nations coming on the horizon. This is obviously very speculative, because no one knows how the world will evolve, but this is the chapter where the first inklings of their success or failure can be explored.

Chapter Summary

In this first chapter, we have addressed what this book is about, who this book is aimed at, the content of the book, and the approach and the philosophy of the book. The following chapters start with some of the foundational concepts in economics that need to be understood, particularly by students. Here, I will be addressing innovation policy, high-tech and complex product systems, and entry barriers. The book then moves on to the specifics of the civil aircraft industry. Finally, it pulls together a framework that will help us decide whether a particular approach is going to be successful in entering the civil aircraft industry.

2.

Foundational Concepts

In this chapter, we will examine the contradictions of some economic theories and practices. The intent of the book is not to address these issues in depth; however, economic theory often creates the underpinning of many people's misconceptions of how a nation or industry develops. The frameworks taught in introductory economics courses start with the idea that a country will develop from a very basic type of agricultural economy and then move through a manufacturing phase, which then will transition into a service economy. This chapter explores several such theories then considers whether they reflect the real world. Chapter 3 talks about industrial policy, which has a similar theme of the contradictions between theory and reality. As we shall see, the widely held view of progression is not preordained.

Because of the general presumption of industry development is along a continuum, we see that many economy planners believe that a transition into civil aircraft manufacturing is inevitable after an economy has conquered other, less technologically challenging, industries. As we will see through the book, however, this concept is untrue. It is very difficult to enter the civil aircraft manufacturing industry for instance.

We are going to look at four subjects in this chapter. First is a theory called the three-sector model, which is the idea that a national economy transitions through various phases. We will explore this in some detail.

The natural development from looking at the three-sector model is to consider the second theory, whether manufacturing is important to a national economy. This is a controversial subject that has been explored expansively in other works.[1] Here, we will consider it in a way that sets the context for why countries aspire to manufacture civil aircraft.

Third, we will consider comparative advantage. This is one of the theoretical underpinnings of global trade. Why do nations excel at certain products, and why are they weak in other areas? As before, this area will be considered with the aim of examining theory versus practice.

Finally, we will address the important area of entry barriers. Given the subject of this book, industry entry barriers will be considered throughout, but in this chapter, we will look specifically at the theoretical concepts.

Review of these four theoretical concepts is relevant to understanding the mindset of policy makers within developing nations that aspire to develop civil aircraft industries. In particular, it will provide context for their mistaken belief that the formation of a civil aircraft industry is inevitable and easy.

We will now address the four issues: the three-sector model, whether manufacturing is important, comparative advantage, and entry barriers. Conclusions will be drawn at the end of the chapter.

The Three-Sector Model

The hypothesis of the three-sector model was developed separately by economists Colin Clark and Jean Fourastié. [2] The model divides a national economy into three sectors of activity:

1. Primary activities include extraction of materials, mining, and direct use of natural resources. Agriculture is also seen as a primary activity of the economy. The theory suggests that countries with very low levels of per capita GDP will be highly skewed to primary activities.

2. Secondary activities are those involved in manufacturing. The secondary sector creates tangible goods and generates wealth by adding value to raw materials and by selling products and services.

3. Tertiary activities are those in the service industry. The tertiary sector produces very little hardware, but people in it provide their knowledge to improve the worth of the economy as a whole, which improves productivity and performance. Many developed economies are highly skewed toward this sector.

The three-sector model is fairly straightforward. Countries with low per capita income today are in the early parts of their national development and produce most of their wealth through the primary sector, typically in agriculture and mining. As nations develop, they start generating their wealth through the secondary sector (i.e., manufacturing), then, progressing further, they eventually rely on the tertiary sector.

The mechanism of progress here is productivity. As productivity starts to improve, people are freed from working in one sector and are enabled to move into the next, and the economy starts generating enough wealth for people to be rich enough to spend money on manufactured goods rather than dedicate their spending to subsistence living (as in a pure agricultural society). Then, as the economy further matures and progresses, productivity improves such that services become a more important part of the economy. These transitions are shown diagrammatically in Chart 2.1.

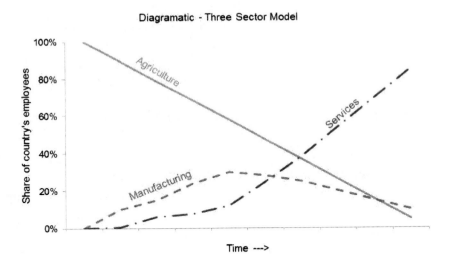

Chart 2.1. Clark's Three-Sector Model

There is a lot of evidence to suggest that this is a fairly robust model. Using data from the US economy going back to the 1850s, we can see employment changes following the patterns as the model would suggest: Agriculture in the 1850s started at about 70% employment of the US economy and transitioned down to 3% or 4% of the economy by the 1980s. Over the same period, the tertiary (services) sector grew from about 18% of the economy to 65% by 2010. The secondary (manufacturing) part of the economy grew from 18% in 1850, peaked at about 30% of the economy in the 1930s and 1940s, and then declined to around 12% of the economy. It is important to remember that we are looking at employment levels rather than industry output, a crucial distinction.

If we consider the output of the economy (e.g., GDP) rather than employment levels, the shifts in the sectors' shares of the economy are not so stark. In terms of employment, the three-sector model appears to predict national development well, but if you look at the output—actual wealth in monetary terms, it is not so clear-cut.

The three-sector model has several weaknesses. First is the belief that development is linear and progressive, but many nations have not progressed that way. This model tends to work well for medium-sized economies but does not work well for less-developed countries where there is a large service sector. For instance, one can think of countries that have jumped straight to a service industry, as in reliance on tourism or financial services.

An area of the three-sector model that I would like to consider further is whether the model works in terms of economic output. The data for sectoral economic output is shown in Chart 2.2. Each data point represents an individual country's position[3]. If we consider very low per capita GDP countries, we see many nations with a high preponderance of GDP generation from agriculture. Anywhere from 20% to 80% of the economy of poor nations can be involved in agriculture. As predicted in the three-sector model, the share reduces rapidly. By the time per capita GDP is around $20,000, agriculture has reduced to 5% of the economy, which is typical of most developed nations.

Agriculture share of world economies

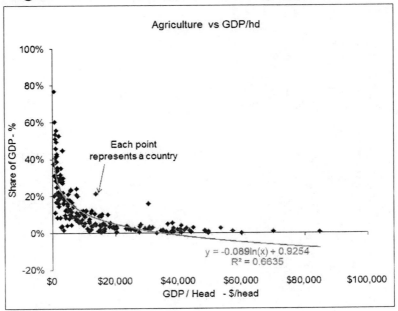

Source: CIA Factbook 2011, GDP(PPP) US$ share for 2011 including estimates

Chart 2.2. Agriculture Sector Share of World Economies

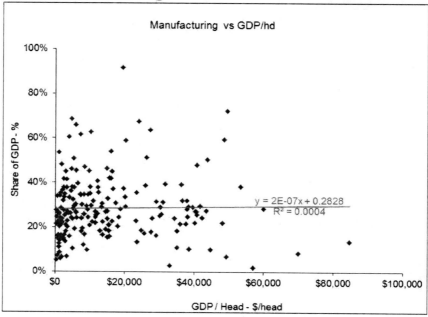

Manufacturing share of world economies

Source: CIA Factbook 2011, GDP(PPP) US$ share for 2011 including estimates

Chart 2.3. Manufacturing Sector Share of World Economies

If we consider the manufacturing share of world economies in terms of output (Chart 2.3), however, the story is not so clear. The data is highly variable. Even with highly developed nations, some countries are very low in the share of GDP to the overall economy, with some as low as 5% and others at 50% or 60%. The theory is thus not so compelling if we look only at manufacturing share.

Service share of world economies

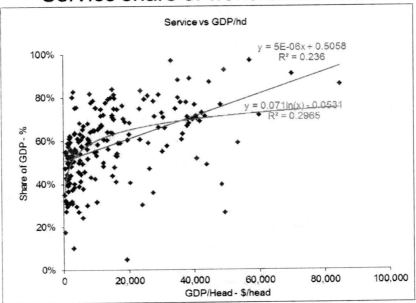

Source: CIA Factbook 2011, GDP(PPP) US$ share for 2011 including estimates

Chart 2.4. Service Sector Share of World Economies

Chart 2.4 shows how the service sector's share moves from a very low level, as the three-sector model predicts, but peaks at around 60% or 70%. Thereafter, once per capita GDP moves above $20,000, the data becomes very variable. There are developed countries with services having 40% of the GDP, and then there are nations with 80%. The three-sector model is therefore not compelling. It works well if we are looking at employment but is not such a strong predictor if we look at things in terms of output (i.e., GPD). To further reinforce this idea, Chart 2.5 groups countries into poor-, low-, medium-, and high-per capita GDP categories.

13

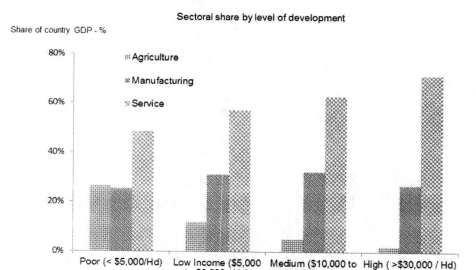

Chart 2.5. Average Sector Shares of World Economies

To further reinforce this in Chart 2.5 I have grouped countries together into four classifications of poor, low, medium, and high-GDP-per-head countries. The manufacturing sector's share of the economy does not deteriorate rapidly as the three-sector model would predict. In fact, it declines very slowly, so in a low-per capita GDP nation, the manufacturing sector's share of GDP is typically around 30%, whereas for high-per capita GDP countries ($30,000 per head), economic output from manufacturing is about 26%.

In the above analysis, I am looking at the average of individual nations, not at the average of the world economy. This is an important caveat because if you look at the United States, which is a major part of the world economy, the manufacturing share is quite low, which would bias the result if you were to think about total world GDP. The point I am trying to make here, however, is that when you are sitting inside an individual nation and making judgements about what your industrial strategy should be, the mix of the economy is at the center of your thinking. Many nations have about 25% of their economy in manufacturing, no matter their wealth. This is an interesting finding.

Where does this bring us to? I think what we can conclude that the three-sector model is a useful starting place for thinking about the evolution of national economies. Generally, as agriculture's share of the economy declines, services increase their share. Interestingly, however, manufacturing appears to be fairly stable throughout in terms of output, though in terms of employment, it is very different.

We thus need to be careful when talking about manufacturing's share of the economy—the important distinction we need to make is whether we are talking about employment or economic output. People can very quickly get into political debate on this subject. Much of the heat in the political discussion is caused by some politicians talking about employment while others are talking about output. It is an important distinction to make because data is different for each one.

A final conclusion about the worth of the three-sector model is that there is a wide variety of manufacturing share even within developed countries. Economies have extremes of share in terms of output: Taiwan, Australia, and Germany have high shares, while the United Kingdom, the United States, and Belgium all have fairly low shares in terms of output. Now let us move on to consider whether manufacturing is important to an economy.

Is Manufacturing Important to an Economy?

Whether manufacturing is important is a live issue generally around the developed world, particularly in the United States and the United Kingdom. Is manufacturing really important to a developed country's national economy? This has been a pressing question since the Great Recession of 2008. There has been a lot of angst in the United States and the United Kingdom over the role of manufacturing and the heavy reliance of those nations on services, particularly financial services.

It is hardly surprising that I, as a worker in the manufacturing industry, strongly believe that manufacturing is important to a nation's economy. I see manufacturing as the mechanism for wealth to be created, rather than moved around, so in full disclosure, let me state that I strongly believe that manufacturing needs to have a good share of an economy to make that economy robust in times of stress, particularly financial stress.

Let us consider the United States, which there is a lot of data. The share of manufacturing in the total workforce has seen a decline, which is an important political consideration in the nation. In 1970, the manufacturing share was around 34% of the economy, and by 2010–2011, it had dropped to 17% or 18%. Why the rapid reduction?

There are two prevailing theories. One is that the nature of manufacturing is productivity and that the result of improved productivity is industry needing fewer people to produce a given amount of output. This is an important part of the decline over the long term of manufacturing's share of the workforce (as the three-sector model would imply).

The alternative theory is that through globalization, manufacturing jobs have been outsourced from the United States to countries were costs of production are lower. This is particularly the case with commoditized products, which lack differentiation and are easily manufactured. The news headlines suggest that a lot of these products (and their associated jobs) have been outsourced to China. There is some element of truth to this rationale, as globalization means freer movement of work across the world and that work can be placed in lower-cost countries.

Commoditization of manufactured goods occurs but is not consistent across all types of manufacturing. Certain types of manufacturing—particularly high-end, high-capital-intensive manufacturing—are still largely carried out in developed nations. Similarly, certain levels of lower-grade manufacturing can be outsourced to places like China. The economic argument is that it is cheaper to ship a part out to China and have value added to that part by a low-cost employee before bringing the part back to the US economy. The economics for this work when you see the total system, but the problem is that when the wages in China increase, the economic calculus may fail to work. In fact, there is some evidence that some parts production is now coming back to the United States from China as China's wage costs have risen.

There is much work, both in academia and in the general business pundit fields, examining this question.[4] This is an important issue. Although I do not want to address it in any great detail in this book, I mention it here because it is a debate within certain circles in civil aircraft manufacturing. The concern is that major aircraft manufacturers have been outsourcing work to lower-cost countries[5]; China comes to mind, as does Mexico. Other nations (e.g., Morocco) are developing a civil aircraft capability. The question becomes whether that is good for the incumbent civil aircraft manufacturer's host nation or good for the aircraft manufacturers themselves in the long term.

Let us get back to "Is manufacturing important?" While manufacturing's share of the workforce has declined in the United States, actual production has gone up. From 1970 to 2011, industrial production output went up 2.5 times. That is remarkable growth, considering that the manufacturing workforce got smaller.

As I said earlier, there are two things going on here: productivity improvement and outsourcing to other nations. The production data captures the output from American companies, but the employment data obviously does not capture those outside the country, so we see manufacturing employment going down quickly while output increases.

There are some important issues here around the question of whether manufacturing is important. Let us explore this a little further. An excellent report entitled "Why Does Manufacturing Matter?" by the Brooking Institution in 2012 addresses this very issue. [6] The Brooking Institution puts forward four major areas in which it believes manufacturing is important. First, the report argues that manufacturing is a very important contributor to environmental concerns and environmental sustainability. In terms of car emissions, for instance, only the manufacturing industry can improve the efficiency of those products and reduce the usage of carbon fuels. Manufacturing not only generates a lot of the environmental problems but also has many of the solutions.

Second, manufacturing of civil aircraft, particularly in the United States, is a major positive contributor to the trade balance. It is one of the only industries in the United States that has a positive manufacturing trade balance, and it is important in that regard, for generating wealth for the nation.

Third, manufacturing typically pays higher-than-average wages. When we look at the average wages of an economy, manufacturing wages tend to be higher than most others. In the United States and Europe, the nature of employees in manufacturing companies are technical people and are typically highly qualified. Companies such as Boeing, General Electric, and other important aircraft industry manufacturers recruit college graduates and people with postgraduate degrees. Because they are highly productive and highly skilled, these employees command high wages. This is good for the nation because these wages are then spent in that economy, which goes on to generate more wealth throughout the nation. This multiplier effect develops as high wage spending cascades through the rest of the economy.

Finally, another area that is profoundly important in my view is that manufacturing is the provider of most innovation within a nation, particularly in the United States. About 70% of company research and development (R&D) is carried out by manufacturing companies. This includes pharmaceutical companies, semiconductor companies, and other manufacturing companies, including Boeing, Pratt & Whitney, Honeywell, and others. Manufacturers are major spenders on innovation. The financial services industry, by comparison, has a low level of R&D and innovation, much lower than in manufacturing.

Why is innovation important? In a mature economy, much of the growth in wealth comes from innovation. GDP has various drivers that make it grow. One of these drivers is demographics. If the population is growing, that naturally produces more GDP. Another driver is investment in capital processes. Here, machines replace people, which improves output. Finally, there is innovation. Many neoclassical economists either understate or do not recognize the role of innovation as a driver of economic growth. If we have a static population and have replaced all the people with machines, growth will be static. The only way to grow GDP is to be innovative and create new products.

We create new products via R&D, which changes the way we do things. In most economies, as mentioned previously, the largest share of R&D is carried out by manufacturing companies. There is a lot of engagement of government, particularly at the front end (the R) of R&D. This activity is often called innovation policy or sometimes industrial policy. As we shall see later, I will argue that the United States has an industrial policy that is very supportive of innovation, which is why we see that country's GDP inexorably improving: There is a large element of innovation driving productivity improvement.

A point not brought out strongly in the Brookings report has been illuminated well by the 2012 report produced by the US president's Advanced Manufacturing Partnership (AMP) Steering Committee. The committee's report published a US Bureau of Economic Analysis study of economic input-output tables. With this analysis, the committee examined the interaction between various industry sectors so we can compare manufacturing to agriculture to construction to transportation and look at the interlinkages between them.

The piece of work that was completed by the AMP Steering Committee investigated the question "What does one dollar of an economic activity generate as a multiplier in the rest of the economy?" One dollar in terms of manufacturing created $1.35, which is a large multiplier. What this means is that if one manufacturing company outputs one dollar, manufacturing draws on many other industries to create its wealth. It takes in raw materials. It takes in energy. It needs construction. It purchases services, such as consultancy, accounting advice, and investment banking. Because of that, manufacturing not only creates wealth intrinsically but also stimulates demand for other industry sectors.

Contrast this with the finance sector, for instance. That sector creates only $0.63. Thus we can see that finance is not a big multiplier in terms of economic activity. It is controversial to say, but that is what the data from the Bureau of Economic Analysis suggests. Intuitively, it makes sense, though. When you think about various states within the United States that have economic-development departments, they always want to have new manufacturing facilities set up in their areas. They subsidize manufacturing companies to come to their states and build factories there. The reason is that higher-paid jobs associated with manufacturing are highly stimulative for the local economy, plus there is the large multiplier effect on other sectors. If you have a manufacturing facility, you will have a lot of connectivity and a lot of multiplier effects that improve your local economy as a whole.

Comparative Advantage

Comparative advantage is one of the economic theories that supports the rationale for international free trade. The original theory was developed by David Ricardo, an English economist, in his work of 1821 called "On the Principles of Political Economy and Taxation."

I do not want to belabor this particular subject, but I do want to explore the inconsistency between the theory of comparative advantage and the reality of international development. First, however, we need to describe the theory. Let us start with an excerpt from an excellent book on global trade by J. Bradford Jensen, who describes the comparative advantage theory eloquently:

> One might think that if a country was capable of producing goods of all types more efficiently than another country, it would not bother to trade with that country. It could produce anything it needed or wanted more cheaply at home. Ricardo showed that the trade even between two such countries can still be beneficial to both, as long as the second country is relatively more efficient at producing some goods. Then, if each country devotes its scarce resources to producing just those goods that it can produce most efficiently, it can sell some of those more cheaply produced goods to the other, freeing up resources in the other country to make what that country produces more efficiently. Each country's inhabitants can then consume more of the goods they desire, and trade thus makes each country better off."[7]

The concept of comparative advantage is captured well in the paragraph above. Essentially, it is a marginal-costs argument. It makes sense for a country to concentrate on things it does well in a relative sense to another country. This is the theoretical underpinning of international trade.

Comparative advantage has a problem: It is based on a static world view. If adopted as a policy, it provides a bleak outlook for a country that has a comparative advantage in low-wage or low-technology goods because it suggests that the country should concentrate in those sorts of goods if the country is trading with a developed nation. This basically dooms the low-wage or low-technology-producing country to having a low per capita GDP. Many countries refuse to accept that this theory is going to be the way forward for them. As a result, they enact policies that will improve their own economies (e.g., import substitution and promotion of exports) and that support and encourage their home industries. This, in a pure Ricardo approach, would not be seen as a good thing to do in the world economy, but the reality is that nations want to improve their relative wealth. They will adopt this stance because that is the nature of the political process within those countries.

Although comparative advantage is a theory, the reality is that in many cases, it is overruled, particularly in developing nations. If we consider developed nations, however, the theory holds a lot of validity. For instance, to a large degree, goods imported into the United States tend to be from low-wage countries supplying lower-technology goods. Apparel, for instance, is an important import; furniture and related products are also important imports to the United States. Exports from the United States tend to be chemicals, transportation equipment, and heavy machinery, which are high-technology goods.

In one sense, then, the theory of comparative advantage holds well but does not take account of the behavioral aspects of decision making in the real world. If you look at it from an individual country's perspective, it is intolerable to think that the country would be doomed to a certain order in the world rankings by virtue of where they are today. Governments will not tolerate that, and they want to move their nations up the value chain of products from where they are, so they want to move from largely agricultural societies into manufacturing, and then eventually into services. They want to improve the wealth of their population.

As with other simplistic economic models, comparative advantage is a useful construct and theory as an introduction to the subject; however, the reality of the world is that countries do not want to stick with the status quo as implied by comparative advantage theory.

Entry Barriers

The analysis of entry barriers was pioneered by the American economist Joseph Bain in 1956.[8] According to Bain, a barrier to entry is anything that places potential new entrants at a competitive disadvantage compared to the incumbents so that established firms are able to earn abnormal profits over the long term. Bain suggested that there are three types of entry barriers: product differentiation, absolute cost advantage, and scale economies. He also argued that the height of the entry barrier determined the magnitude of long-term profits for incumbents.

The subject of abnormal profits is controversial. Bain's neoclassical economics stance is that firms collude more readily in concentrated markets. Entry barriers are relevant because firms will regard collusion as worthwhile only where there are barriers preventing rapid erosion of collusion profits. The traditional approach would therefore anticipate a positive statistical relationship between concentration, barriers to entry, and profitability.

An alternative theory, put forward by Demsetz in 1973, suggests that the high profits in concentrated markets could simply be indicative of greater efficiency. This debate continues within the economics field and will not be examined any further in this book, although Bain's basic premise of three types of entry barriers is worthy of further examination.

Product Differentiation

Bain's first barrier arises from the existing firms having established products that have built up customer goodwill. Although new entrants may be capable of producing functionally similar products at a similar cost, they will be at a disadvantage because they must either spend more on advertising or reduce their price to gain sales from the current customer base.

A preference for an incumbent's product is created by the cost of making buying decisions. Consumers must acquire information to make a choice among products whose benefits cannot be discovered by inspection prior to acquisition (sometimes known as experienced goods). These costs are known as sunk costs. It may be costly for them to reevaluate the purchase choices with the arrival of every new product on to the market, and as a consequence, new entrants will incur additional costs of generating sales in the form of discounts or high advertising expenditure to overcome consumer-switching costs to achieve their sales target.

Absolute Cost Advantage

Patents, access to superior resources, and lower cost of finances are typical sources of absolute cost advantage. This type of barrier exists "if the prospective unit costs of production of potential entrant firms are generally—and more or less at any common scale of operations—higher than those of established firms" (Bain, 1956).

Absolute cost advantages arise when new entrants must use inferior techniques or pay higher prices for product components or raw materials that may be caused by actions of incumbents. Alternatively, asymmetries between incumbents and new entrants can be created when incumbents exploit superior technology protected by patents. A patent gives a legally enforceable right to prevent others from using an invention for a specific number of years. The rationale is that it provides the incentive to innovate because it slows the speed of imitation. Applying for patents is a way by which a firm can deliberately delay the arrival of competitors; in short, the aim of patents is to create government-authorized monopolies.

Another way of looking at cost advantage was proposed by Jacobides,[9] who proposed three forms of cumulative advantage for incumbent firms, which also provide absolute cost advantages. First, he proposed that incumbent firms can benefit from already having factories because suggestions for innovations can be collected from a large and well-informed employee base.

Second, cumulativeness is reliant on the existence of tacit knowledge. The innovation process within a firm is tacit when (1) knowledge cannot easily be copied or transferred, (2) knowledge is space- and time-dependent, and (3) entrants have a difficult task in replicating the innovations. Tacit knowledge is often a feature of newly developing industries, where progress is based on on-the-spot experimentation rather than on understanding of underlying principles.

The systemic component of innovation is Jacobides' final reason for cumulativeness. In complex product systems (see Chapter 4), it is often the case that innovations take place in subsystems. The advantage an incumbent has is that it will be able to understand the interactions of such subsystems that innovation has with the whole of the complex product system.

Jacobides argues that "the more a particular industry is characterized by the production of big, complex, non-decomposable systems, the more cumulative the innovation, and less entering firms and entrepreneurial ventures will succeed". This view has great relevance to the civil aircraft sector.

Scale Economies

Entrants can experience economies of scale through what is known as the percentage effect and through the absolute capital requirements effect. The percentage effect depends on the minimum efficient scale of production relative to the market. It is particularly pertinent when the former is a large fraction of the industry size (typified by the civil aircraft industry). If an entrant decides to enter the market at an inefficient scale, the move is likely to reduce prices. This need to enter the market at a relatively high production level is particularly important in industries that have large fixed costs or high unit volumes. If the entrant enters at a less than efficient scale, it will face a cost penalty. In either case, the entrant is at a disadvantage.

An absolute capital requirement effect also arises from difficulties in financing, which are likely to be large investments in the case of civil aircraft. As these outlays will be large and the impact on the market entry uncertain, an entrant may suffer an absolute cost disadvantage. This is because financial institutions see the entrant as a higher risk and will therefore charge higher interest rates than for incumbents.

How Entry Costs Change as Industries Develop

The three types of barriers to market entry put forward by Bain have been developed within the context of a neoclassical economic framework, and although very useful, they lack a dynamic component. Are entry barriers the same at the beginning of an industry as those at the end? Mueller and Tilton[10] examined this issue. They broke down the industry cycle into four stages: innovation, imitation, technological competition, and standardization.

They argued that entry at the innovation and imitation stages is relatively easy but becomes difficult at the technological-competition stage. This is because initial innovation and resultant experimentation tend to be done by small entrepreneurial companies who are willing to take high risks for potential high reward. As the number of firms entering the industry increases and more R&D is undertaken on innovation, the scientific and technological frontiers of technology expand rapidly. Research becomes specialized, and the technology gets broken down into its constituent parts, with individual research focusing on improvements of small elements of the technology. By the technology-competition stage, most firms in the industry are carrying out extensive R&D programs, and small firms outside the industry find it difficult to enter and establish R&D efforts that can compete effectively with incumbents.

In addition to this economy-of-scale problem, the entrant faces a heavy initial investment in R&D required to bring the firm up to date technologically. This is because the amount of uncodified knowledge the incumbents may have is substantial (i.e., an absolute cost advantage).

Finally, in the standardization stage, the industry slows and technologies become standardized and patents have expired. Barriers remain but are more concentrated on efficient production and competition is moved from innovation to price.

Based largely on empirical studies, Mueller and Tilton argued persuasively of the dynamic nature of entry barriers; however, they still utilized many of the essential elements of Bain's static framework, because his framework has proven to be remarkably robust and is cited extensively in the literature.[11]

In this book, the relevant elements of the framework from both Bain's and Mueller and Tilton's work on entry barriers, coupled with my own experience, will be used to illuminate the features of the civil aircraft industry.

Conclusion: Economic Foundations

If we draw together the themes of the three-sector model, whether manufacturing is important to an economy, comparative advantage, and entry barriers, we can conclude that it is not inevitable that manufacturing will decline in share of the value created in an economy. Employee numbers may reduce as the economy grows in terms of per capita GDP, but this is the nature of the constant productivity improvement in manufacturing. Inevitably, it seems that employment will decline in the long run. For many economies, that is a worrisome trend, but it seems to be a reality.

I do want to reinforce, however, that the decline of manufacturing in terms of output is not inevitable. In fact, one could argue that such decline can be managed. In certain countries, manufacturing is highly valued as a part of the economy and managed to ensure that it is a large proportion of the economy. One country that comes to mind is Germany, where manufacturing is actively encouraged and policies, networks, and structures support manufacturing. Some would argue that Germany benefits from a more robust economy and can withstand economic shocks well.

Another conclusion that arises from the discussion in this chapter is that manufacturing is important. We looked at the Brookings work, which suggests that various aspects of manufacturing are essential to a nation. If a country wants to improve the wealth of its population, it needs to be innovative and highly developed at the technological frontier. The only way to do this is to have an adequate flow of new products and services that can grow GDP.

The theory of comparative advantage works in an isolated sense but is static. The world is always developing, so if a nation wants to move up the value chain, it will do things that, to the eyes of a fundamental believer of the theory of comparative advantage, would seem unsound. Countries have aspirations. They want to develop wealth for their populations; they want to improve themselves so governments will inevitably deploy industrial policies. There is no escaping the fact that we do not live in a theoretical world; we live in the real world, and people have aspirations to improve themselves.

Entry barriers will be a recurring theme though this book. As we progress, we will appreciate that civil aircraft manufacturing has high entry barriers. It is very difficult to enter the industry because the product is complex and the interactions of the various subsystems within the product are very hard to understand. Later, as we look at entry barriers from various aspects, we will see commercial reasons that make entry into the civil aircraft industry difficult. For example, the sheer magnitude of investment required to develop an aircraft is high (billions of dollars) and often underestimated.

Geopolitical aspects also create entry barriers to this industry. One can imagine that certain nations aspire to civil aircraft production purely for the reason that it creates spin-off defense technology that enables them to compete in a geopolitical sense against the United States and Europe. We will be examining these concepts in more detail later. The corollary of this is that some nations, because they are protected by the United States, have been held back because they do not need a large indigenous military aircraft-manufacturing industry, which holds them back in civil aircraft development. We will explore some of those issues as we go through the book.

In the next chapter, I address innovation and industrial policy. It is essential that we explore them so we can understand why countries do the things they do and aspire to develop new industries at the technological frontier.

3.

Innovation, Industrial Policy, and Government Support

In this chapter, we are going to consider the subject of innovation and the closely aligned area of industrial policy. This will naturally lead us into exploring the role of government and its intervention in various guises in the industry of civil aircraft, which, as we will see, is a theme throughout this book. These subjects are important to the success of civil aircraft manufacturing industries.

Innovation is at the heart of a globally competitive civil aircraft industry. A manufacturer has to create a product that is at the technological frontier. Boeing and Airbus compete with one another at the technological frontier and make significant financial investments to ensure that their products are really leading-edge.

We will also explore the subject of invention and the difference between it and innovation. We will consider a framework for looking at innovation, as well as how companies manage innovation. These subjects are crucial to leading companies such as Airbus, Boeing, Bombardier, and Embraer.

Industrial policy has political connotations, particularly in the United States and, to a lesser extent, in the United Kingdom. In both countries, industrial policy is often seen through the lens of picking winners and losers, meaning that governments are making decisions about whether companies win or lose in a financial sense. As we will see, this is a simplistic perspective. The United States and the United Kingdom governments are heavily involved in industrial policy as are most others. We will explore this subject in detail.

Edison: Invention, Innovation, and Government

Let us start with the subject of innovation. As an introduction to this subject, I thought it would be useful to consider the US icon Thomas Edison.[1] Most people have the idea that Edison was a great inventor and had more than 1,000 patents to his name. The reality, however, is that he was an innovator. To consider this further, let us examine one of his most famous claims to fame: the "invention" of the lightbulb.[2]

Although Edison patented the lightbulb in 1878, the idea of a lightbulb was developed in 1802 by Sir Humphry Davy in the United Kingdom, where he had demonstrated the basic principle of a filament being used to illuminate. The concept was then iterated and developed through the years, and by 1860, Joseph Swan demonstrated the use of carbonized filaments in a glass bulb evacuated of air. That was close to the design that Edison eventually patented.

Edison brought the whole concept together and, most importantly, brought it to market and protected it via a patent. An often-quoted passage from Edison is relevant here: "Make it a practice to keep on the lookout for novel and interesting ideas that others have used successfully. ... Your idea has to be original only in its adaptation to the problem you are working on."

Going a little deeper into Edison's life story is instructive. This could take a whole book, but we are just going to look at some of the major milestones in his life related to the electrical industry. We will then draw lessons from his approach to innovation.

Edison was born in 1847. By 1869, he had his first patent for an electric vote recorder. As I said earlier, in 1878, he patented the first incandescent light. Then by the early 1880s, he had various patents for a system of electrical distribution and applied to New York for permission to build the nation's first electrical power station. At that time, gas was the major illuminator for people's homes. As one can imagine, there was a lobby against his plans for electricity, but New York eventually granted him permission to build the first national power station.

Edison had patents, which meant a monopoly on electrical lighting and his approach for electrical power distribution. He moved quickly and installed a base of power stations in the New York area, and by 1883, he had more than three hundred in operation. Soon after this rapid growth, however, was the so-called Current War, which was the battle between alternating current and direct current, the two ways to generate and transmit electricity. Edison was an advocate for direct current and was on the losing side of the optimal solution. Today, we still have alternating current coming through the electrical outlets in our homes because it is a more efficient way to distribute electricity than the direct-current approach.

Another facet of this story is that Edison's first activities were funded by J. P. Morgan and the Vanderbilt family. By the time he was in the midst of the Current War, Edison had a large company over which there was a battle for ownership. Eventually, in the late 1880s, J. P. Morgan won 40% of the company and Thomas Edison settled for a 10% stake. Edison then exited the power-distribution and lighting industry, and his company, which would eventually become General Electric.

The issue I would like to draw attention to here is the role of government. First of all, Edison was granted patents, which are bestowed by governments. Basically, the government allows a patent holder to have monopoly profits. Second, New York allowed and gave Edison the authorization to build his power plant. Without that authorization and that encouragement to go forward with an innovative product, he would have been struggling.

Another later aspect of government engagement is interesting. During the 1920s, vertical integration was seen as enabling companies to gouge[3] (i.e., charge very high prices), so General Electric exited the utilities business because of an antitrust action by the US government. Later, in the 1940s, the company was forced to release some of its lightbulb patents to other companies.

What we learn here is that the innovator is allowed to participate in the market and allowed to have monopoly profits but the government can take privileged market access away, as we saw at the end of the story of Edison's creation. The notion that the private individual can go off on his own and make things happen is a misapprehension.

Innovation and Invention

Next, let us consider the difference between invention and innovation. Invention is the use and creation of something for the first time. It is the creation of a product, an idea, or a concept for the first time ever. Innovation is different, however. Innovation is bringing an idea to the marketplace and making it saleable and useable. Innovation always builds on something—typically on several inventions or other innovations[4].

Invention is often mistaken for innovation, but they are very different ideas. Invention is rare. Examples of the creation of something brand new are exceptional, whereas innovation pervades most products, particularly in high-tech manufacturing. Innovation is at the heart of most companies, which integrate various technologies and slowly, incrementally improve the resultant product.

One way of looking at innovation is in terms of radical innovation and incremental innovation. The framework we will utilize is the so-called hill-climbing paradigm.[5] Chart 3.1 shows a conception of their model.

Degree of novelty – incremental or radical

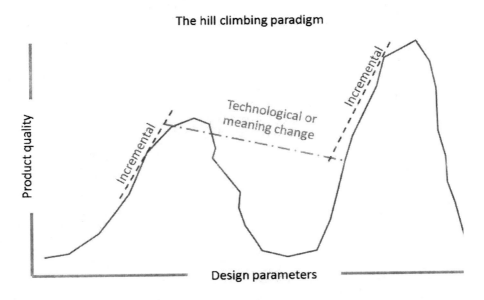

The hill climbing paradigm

Norman, D & Verganti (2014), Incremental and radical innovation: Design versus technology and meaning change, Design Issues, pp 30(1) 78-96

Chart 3.1. Degree of Novelty (Incremental or Radical): The Hill-Climbing Paradigm

We can imagine two adjacent mountains, one higher than the other, and a group of climbers who are moving up the smaller mountain in a slow, steady way. This is analogous to incremental innovation. The top of the mountain represents the end of the line for a technology, where no more improvements can be made. Examples in aircraft manufacturing are the timber-built aircraft before the First World War or the piston-engine aircraft that were used to the end of the Second World War.

Sooner or later, a technology plateaus and there is not much more improvement to be made. That is usually when a radical innovation comes along. This is analogous to the climbers moving to the next mountain, which is higher. Once on that mountain they start incrementally climbing it.

Essentially, radical innovation is a big jump in terms of change—a big change of technology or process. For the most part, however, companies are involved in incremental innovation. In fact, much research has been done on this and suggests that in most companies, 80% to 90% of their time is spent on incremental innovation. This is particularly true of aerospace but is true of most other industries too.

If we look at the research and development (R&D) expenditures of most companies, we see that most of the expenditures are on incremental innovation, which is a small, steady improvement of a current product. This can be seen in aircraft manufacturing. Throughout history, there has been a steady improvement in efficiency of aircraft and jet engines. It is quite unusual to see a radical change; it does happen, of course, but it is unusual.

Management of Innovation in Firms

Most engineering and manufacturing companies have rigorous management processes to handle incremental innovation.[6] These processes usually take the form of progression through gated reviews. There is the idea of a hierarchy of technology starting from something that is very basic and unproven to something that has been well proven in testing and demonstrated. This can be considered a continuum of level-of-technology readiness.

Companies manage their technology through that continuum. One of the most favored frameworks in the aerospace industry is a hierarchy called the National Aeronautics and Space Administration (NASA) technology readiness level (TRL). This is a standard definition produced by NASA. Basically, each technology level can be given a position on the continuum, which ranges from TRL 1, which is very basic research, to TRL 9, which is a technology that has been fully tested.

Many companies adopt a policy to use only technologies that have reached a certain TRL level. It could be TRL 5 or 6. The company will manage technologies through the hierarchy until the technology reaches the end, though in some cases, it may never reach the end. It may fail in its testing and examination and may therefore not be embodied in a product.

The mindset of mature engineering organizations tends to be focused on incremental innovation, though companies also manage radical innovation. Typically, a company has a small division that is isolated from the traditional engineering organization. The engineers and scientists in this part of the organization will carry out the more radical work. Lockheed's famous Skunk Works epitomizes this concept. Most companies in aerospace have a similar entity that does these sorts of advanced programs, with many of these advanced programs being defense-related.

Another aspect of management of radical innovation in aerospace companies is the idea of linkage with universities. Many companies have networks of linkages to universities. Academic institutions are a lot freer thinking, so to speak, than companies and have a lot more freedom to think outside the box.

There is recognition within companies that managing radical innovation is different from managing incremental innovation. Both are very important to a company, as radical innovation is very long-term in its outlook and incremental innovation is more short-term.

While on the subject, let us take a short diversion to explore the subject of measuring innovation. We need to address a few misconceptions relevant to the ongoing debate of the competitiveness of nations.

Measuring Innovation

Innovation is very difficult to measure. Most lay individuals imagine that R&D expenditures and number of patents are measures of innovation, but these are only measures of the *inputs* to innovation, not of outputs. Similarly, we see much said in the popular press about the number of engineers and scientists coming out of universities in the West when compared to, say, China and other nations in the Far East in an alarming way. It is difficult to obtain an accurate measure of innovation as an output. For instance, it would be very helpful to be able to measure the quality of engineers and scientists graduating from universities as well as the number, but this is a difficult metric to assess.

The only area I have seen that actually addresses this issue is a publication by the Organisation for Economic Co-operation and Development (OECD), a multi-government think tank, in 2010, entitled "Measuring Innovation: A New Perspective." One of the most useful charts in the report is on the subject of highly cited scientific articles. This chart shows the United States to have nearly 50% of all highly cited scientific works. This is important because when an academic piece of work will get published, the relevant measure is whether it is cited by other scientists. This is an excellent metric for showing the academic paper's relevance to scientific understanding moving forward. If other academics cite a paper, it is seen as having value. This analysis by the OECD suggests that nearly half of all the highly cited academic papers in the world are produced by the United States' scientists, which contrasts sharply with the high production rate of China's academia, which has low citation counts for its papers.

I do not have a solution for measuring innovation output, but I do think a good metric is the measure of academic paper citations. In that world ranking, we have the United States at nearly at 50%, the United Kingdom at 14%, Germany at about 12%, France at 6%, and China at just 6%.

After this brief excursion into the difficulty of measuring innovation output, we now return to the broader theme of national involvement in stimulating the activity.

National Systems of Innovation

At this point, we need to consider systems of national innovation. Much academic work has been carried out in this field,[7] and it is important to think about linkage of economic performance of countries and how they innovate.

What do we mean by a national innovation system? There are many definitions, but essentially, a national innovation system is the structure of institutions within a nation that addresses innovation. These could be in the private sector or in government. Those institutions interact to stimulate and foster technology development.

Let me cite an example to try to explain this. As Freeman (1995) notes, Japan in the 1970s had a strong producer and subcontractor network and linkages within the country—one could imagine car companies having extremely good linkages to their subcontractor networks—whereas the Union of Soviet Socialist Republics (USSR, which was a communist nation at the time) had weak or nonexistent linkages between marketing, production, and procurement of services. This is a weakness because important interaction is not occurring between suppliers, the supply chain, and users. Such interaction is an element of an innovation system. In contrast we have the idea that Japan was highly exposed to international competition during the 1970s. At this time, the Japanese economy was growing rapidly, particularly through cars and information technology (IT) industries growth, but the USSR very little exposure to the international markets at the time, so their products were weak in international comparisons.

This whole subject is broad; there are many people having many different perspectives on it. At its fundamental level, however, is the notion that structurally within a nation, how universities interact with companies, and how those companies interact with their customers and their supply chains can have a profound effect on how well the countries innovate.

There is a lot of academic work on this, so we will not explore it in a theoretical way further. The subject of national innovation systems will serve as a backdrop when we examine various countries' individual performance in the production of civil aircraft, however.

Industrial Policy

A nation's industrial policy is an important part of the success or failure of an indigenous civil aircraft industry. If there is a supportive industrial policy within the nation, it is highly likely that civil aircraft manufacturing will be successful. Similarly, certain industrial policy regimes can hold back a civil aircraft industry from developing.

In this section, I will explain some of the basic concepts of industrial policy. First, let us define industrial policy. Industrial policy can be defined as a specific effort by a nation to encourage the development of the manufacturing sector in that country. The idea is that the government decides how to allocate resources and makes decisions about which sectors are going to succeed and the mechanisms by which it is going to support those sectors. These mechanisms are usually not specific to a specific company, though in civil aircraft production, it is sometimes inevitable, given the structure of the industry.

One of the best frameworks in terms of trying to understand industrial policy is put forward by Ferguson and Ferguson (1994). They conceptualize a matrix that classifies whether a policy has one of four classifications:

- Laissez-faire—This is essentially a free-market conception of the market. Information flows are perfect, and participants act rationally, driven by self-interest. With these conditions, there is no need for industrial policy; the market is left to decide.

- Supportive—Here, there is recognition that there are occasions when information flow is not perfect and the market is not totally perfect, but for the most part, they are. On those occasions when there are some market failures, however, the government can intervene.

- Active—As defined by Ferguson and Ferguson, a policy that is active has a much more direct selection of industries that need to be supported in a strategic conception of what is good for the country.

- Planning—This type of policy is associated with the now-failed model of communism. This is a centralized planning government allocating resources centrally, with no notion that the market allocates optimally at all.

The categories above are one dimension of the Ferguson matrix. The other dimension is the policy's intended outcome:

- Neutral—There is no engagement, so it is a free market.

- Accelerative—Any actions carried out by the home government are to accelerate innovation within the nation.

- Decelerative—This is a more controversial aspect of a policy. It is the idea of helping companies or sectors that are failing. Here, the market has moved on or a foreign competitor is much cheaper, and that is causing the home industry to fail. Decelerative policy is usually cast as short-term support for an industry to handle a transition. The aim is to restructure the industry or company from being in economic distress to being successful.

Let me cite some examples to explore the insights from the Ferguson and Ferguson framework. In a classic view of the United States, the country's industry policy is one of laissez-faire: There is no intervention, so there is naturally no funding going into specific sectors. That is highly questionable in reality, and a lot of recent work has been done to disabuse ourselves of the notion that the United States has no industrial policy.

Mariana Mazzucato's book *The Entrepreneurial State* [8] and work by Fred Block on the rise of the developmental state in the United States[9] are very good revelations about the real nature of the extent that the US government supports industries. The aerospace industry is one of the beneficiaries of this, and there are others, such as pharmaceuticals, who are large recipients of the heavy hand of government in the United States.

An example of accelerative support is investment in a targeted industry. The classic example of active investment is Japan's Ministry of International Trade and Industry (MITI) activities in the 1970s and 1980s to stimulate automobile and IT industry development. Similarly, Brazil provided early and sustained support to enable the success of the indigenous civil aircraft company Embraer, which now competes effectively in the global market.

On the decelerative side, we see support for industries such as Germany's shipbuilding industry and the coal and iron industry within the European Union. These required substantial financial help to transition into becoming more competitive against competition from the Far East.

In summary, industrial policies can be classified in various ways, ranging from very little engagement by government through pure communism (letting the state allocate all resources).

Rationales for Government Intervention

We need to accept that governments intervene. We are not in a world where governments accept laissez-faire markets, even in the United States. There is nowhere where governments do not interfere in the marketplace. Governments are particularly active at the technological frontier, and their engagement is widespread. There are several rationales for government intervention, which we will consider in this section.

Public Good

Government intervention theory starts with the Economics 101 course perspective of a public good. The idea is that something will not be made if left to the marketplace but really needs to be completed for society as a whole. From a national perspective, the classic case is having an army, building a defense capability, and having an armaments industry. If left to the marketplace, these would not happen because there would be little incentive for private companies to do that, so the state is involved to fund these efforts and to manage the defense of the country. That is what is termed a public good.

Similarly, the rollout of an education system, particularly in the United States in the early 20th century would be seen as a public good. Infrastructure is another good example, including the building out of road and railway systems.[10] Left to the market, these things would not be deployed in the nation, though the nation needs them to develop a modern economy.

Capital Market Failure

The concept of capital market failure is similar to that of public good. For example, a technology that shows promise but is a long way from being brought to market within a laissez-faire environment is unlikely to get funding. Capital markets are not perfect. They are run by individuals, and individuals have a high risk threshold. If they do not see a fairly short-term return, the reality is, money will probably not be made available for risky technologies. This is where the role of government comes in; the government would take the risk to fund that industry for the benefit of the country as a whole.

Strategic Trade Theory

This is a very particular aspect in terms of international competition. Paul Krugman, an economist, was one of the people who did some of the early work on this in the 1980s. [11] The best example of this is the creation of Airbus in Europe. In the 1970s, the United States was increasingly successful in world markets with its civil aircraft from Boeing; meanwhile, the fragmented European domestic industries of the United Kingdom, France, Germany, and Italy were failing. It was the European governments' intervention that orchestrated the creation of Airbus. The idea was to create a competitor that would have a scale and capability that could compete against Boeing. To make this happen, the European companies had to have government funding. There was a lot of government funding for Airbus in the early years, and it was justified under the notion of strategic trade theory. From Europe's perspective, the United States, and Boeing in particular, was a monopoly supplier of civil aircraft and the European airlines were likely to be gouged by the America monopoly supplier, so it made sense for them to create their own competitor. The policy was to create a competitive dynamic that made sure that European airlines were not being overcharged by a US airframer. The other benefit of this strategy was that it saved high-paying technology jobs in each of those nations in Europe. It thus had a large social component to it as well as a strategic trade aspect.

Job Protection

Another rationale for government intervention is job protection. Individuals have voting power, and if they lobby their governments to stop foreign competition, they sometimes succeed by establishing funding to support industries that are uncompetitive if left to their own devices.

Leveling the Playing Field

A slight nuance of the job-protection rationale is the leveling-the-playing-field argument, as it is called. Here, the idea is that a country needs subsidies to compete because other nations unfairly subsidize their home industries. Some countries rationalize their support of their own industries because it is the only way their industries can compete with industries supported by their nations. There are nations that compete with the United States that say, "The United States spends a lot of money on defense, and that defense R&D support is helpful for their civil sector. We do not have a defense sector, so the only way we can compete is to fund our civil sector to compensate for the United States' advantage." That is a typical leveling-the-playing-field argument.

Technology Diffusion

Two rationales for government support are more prevalent in developing countries than in developed nations. First is technology diffusion. According to this notion, some industries have very good track records of introducing technology that can be spun off or diffused to the rest of the economy, which brings the whole nation up in terms of capability.

Aerospace is an industry with high technology-diffusion characteristics. Some nations specifically fund and structure their support for the aerospace industry because it has excellent technology diffusion, and these nations see one of the reasons for funding aerospace as improving the nation as a whole.

Industrial Targeting

A reason for government support different from diffusion is that of national pride: A nation wants to make sure that it has a place at the international high-technology table, so it funds a high-technology company. This is industrial targeting. The nation sees the broader economic benefit in a way similar to that of technology diffusion, but in a different guise. Basically, industrial targeting is a national-champion consideration.

Summary of types of government intervention

Above, we have considered several rationales for government intervention. Later in this book, we will explore several countries and how they rank against these various considerations and rationales. Some countries have strong public-good and strategic-trade-theory rationales to support their aircraft industries. Other nations are explicit about job protection and leveling the playing field.

Before we close this chapter, it is instructive to briefly examine the route by which some of our technology icons achieved their fame. As we will see, many received help from the government in the early days of their efforts.

Government Role with Innovation Icons

The role of government is omnipresent in most economies. Many icons of innovation have had the help of government to create their successes. This is particularly the case in their early stages, when they were seen as high-risk innovators and no private individuals or companies wanted to invest in them.

Let me cite three examples. First is the enabling of Google. Both Lawrence Page and Sergey Brin's original research for the algorithm used by Google to rank Internet websites was funded by the National Science Foundation through a grant and a fellowship. The intellectual property rights (IPR) are owned by Stanford University, so while Page Rank is a trademark of Google, the patent is assigned to Stanford University. Google has exclusive rights to the patent and pays a fee to Stanford for its use. This goes back, of course, to the early days when the original concept was developed and was a government-funded activity. Now the company has gone on to great things, but the initial high-risk funding was actually paid for by the US government.

Another high-profile innovation of recent importance is oil fracking. This is the technique of hydraulically fracking shale deposits to release oil and gas from deep below the earth's surface. Far from being a private innovation, this industry has had the benefit of government-funded activity. In the 1970s, the Department of Energy and industry gas-research institutes were funding research into this area. The research was then adopted by various companies to deploy in the field, but the initial concepts and design rules were funded by the US government.

Finally, one of the greatest icons of our time, a technology product icon, is the iPhone from Apple. An excellent piece of work done by Mariana Mazzucato in her book *The Entrepreneurial State* [12] deconstructs the iPhone contributing technologies. The product's technological roots can be traced back to the Department of Energy, the Department of Defense, various US military programs, Defense Advanced Research Projects Agency (DARPA), and Army research. Most, if not all, of these technologies that have been assembled by Apple in the iPhone originated somewhere else— the government. It was not Apple that invented these technologies or brought them to fruition. Apple packaged them into something that was highly attractive to customers, but the actual technologies were funded by government.

These are three examples, but there are many more. The persuasive narrative that many people believe is that private industry is highly successful in terms of innovation. Often, however, the roots of successful innovation lie in government intervention.

Chapter Summary

This chapter briefly explored innovation, industrial policy, and the role of government in industry. Innovation is different from invention, and various countries take different attitudes toward encouraging innovation. They enact their different views through industrial policy. Certain industrial policies can be very successful in terms of encouraging a globally competitive civil aircraft industry, though other industrial policies can be bad at making sure that countries have companies that can compete on the world stage.

We will consider these issues in detail at the individual country level later on in the book. In the next chapter we will examine the nature of the products, competing at the technology frontier, and how globalization is allowed to happen.

4.

High-Technology Products

In this last chapter covering the foundational aspects of this book, we are going to consider the product itself in a generic form. This will lead into the next section, which addresses more closely the civil aircraft industry, but it is important to step back at this stage to explore the nature of high technology and, in the process, put away some misconceptions about the subject.

We are going to be discussing three general areas in this chapter. First, we will address the issue of the technology frontier and what it is. Second, we will consider the area of complex products. Finally, we will explore the controversial subject of whether globalization in high technology is inevitable.

The Technological Barrier

Let me first define what I mean by the "technological barrier." One can imagine that there are various technologies and approaches to product innovation. One approach is copying somebody else's products or making small minor changes to others' products. At the other extreme is innovation of products.

By "technological barrier" or "technological frontier," I mean products that require high levels of development and high levels of innovative, creative thought to bring a product concept to the marketplace. This is a different phenomenon from "catch-up technology" prevalent in developing nations. In its crudest sense, catch-up technology is copying; someone else has made the major breakthrough in an innovative technology, and the catch-up country's strategy is essentially to copy it. This makes perfect sense for a country at the early stage of its development, when jumping straight to the technological frontier is not feasible. The approach is very useful in developing nations as they aim to fast-track their catch-up with developed nations.

The problem with the catch-up approach is that sooner or later as a country moves up in capability, it runs out of technologies to copy. At this point, the country finds that it is at the technological barrier.

Competing at the technological barrier requires a different method of innovation. Creativity and broad, deep knowledge of adjacencies in terms of technology is important. It has been found that it is difficult for nations to navigate the transition from a copying strategy to competing with new technology created indigenously.[1]

Clearly, developed nations are essentially at the technological barrier. The leading civil aircraft manufacturers Airbus, Boeing, Bombardier, and Embraer have high levels of research and development (R&D) because they compete at the technological barrier and are pushing forward through it to create new product advantages.

Why do nations try to transition to innovation at the technological barrier? They have transitioned from having low wage economies to high-wage economies. They often find themselves uncompetitive, and their GDP growth rates falter. If they do not restructure their economies, they will fall into a trap known by economists as the middle-income gap.

There are many examples of countries that have seen very rapid growth in terms of GDP and particularly of per capita GDP and then have slowed or stopped growing because they have not managed to transition their economies into leading-edge economies.

Justin Lin, the former chief economist at the World Bank, puts it very well in his book *The Quest for Prosperity*:

> When the latecomer's income reaches about half the income of advanced countries—or about $20,000 in today's dollars—it finds it more difficult to identify industries likely to be consistent with its latent comparative advantage. Most of its industries are on or close to the global frontier, and industrial upgrading and diversification rely increasingly on indigenous innovations, not simply on copying successful examples from abroad. In that situation, policies to support

industrial upgrading and diversification begin to resemble those of advanced countries and carry much higher risks of failure.[2]

Another passage from Lin is particularly instructive:

> Many of them have not engineered the structural evolution for advancing most of their industries to the global technological frontier and competing head-to-head with other developed companies, except in a few sectors. In concrete economic terms, the middle-income trap is a slowing of growth and structural changes as economies are caught between low-wage manufacturers and high-wage innovators.

I address this subject in this book because, as we will see later, some countries believe that the continuum of technological development is linear and progression is straightforward. That is not the case in reality, however. Although copying is an efficient strategy for moving quickly up the value chain, there is a real step change to competing at the technological barrier.

As we will see later, some countries have not managed to reach the barrier while some countries are approaching it. There are big questions about whether they will have the wherewithal to change their economies to compete at the technological barrier.[3]

High Technology and Complex Products

Similarly to how nations consider technological development a linear path, most of us not involved in the innovation field perceive that products are on a linear continuum. Again, this is not the case. There is a whole classification of products, which are not covered well by academia, called complex product systems, or CoPS for short.

Before we address CoPS, let us contrast two high-technology products. Consider the quintessential Apple iPhone that many of us have. The iPhone is considered by most to be a high-technology product but is very different from a jet aircraft, which would also be classified by most to be a high-technology product.

Let us look at the characteristics of these products. The iPhone will last four to five years and then will be essentially obsolete. iPhones, even though they are extremely reliable, do sometimes fail to initiate an application (app), but the consequences of failure of an iPhone are not particularly dire. It would be highly unusual for someone to be injured if an iPhone app failed to open.

Contrast the challenge in designing an iPhone with that for designing a jet aircraft. Typically, an aircraft from Boeing or Airbus will last for twenty years or longer in revenue-generating service. An aircraft has a punishing regime throughout its life. It flies 4,000 to 5,000 hours a year, with multiple takeoffs and landings in a day, which puts tremendous stress on the whole aircraft structure. The environment in which the aircraft flies is stringent, from extreme colds to high temperatures and from low to very high atmospheric pressures. The machine has to lift tons of its own weight upward, as well as the passengers and their baggage. It has to create essentially its own breathable environment at 35,000 feet. The design task is made even more challenging because the consequences of failure are immense, so the safety-critical systems onboard are duplicative and triplicative in many cases so that if one system fails, another can back it up.

An aircraft is a remarkable machine. It is frustrating for us in the industry for people to not recognize the fantastic technological achievement that it is. The problem is that an aircraft is so reliable and robust that people do not recognize it for what it is: an exceptionally safe and dependable high-technology product that makes the world a smaller place.

There are further differences between iPhones and CoPS, generally. Complex products are low-volume, very-high-capital goods machines, and their design is highly collaborative in terms of the interaction with customers.

Unlike consumer goods, the chronological progression for the creation of CoPS is sell, develop, and then produce. First, a company needs to sell the product in concept to the operator. Then the manufacturer makes a risk-assessed judgment that it can develop the product. It believes it knows enough about the systems and their interactions and has confidence that it knows how the aircraft will perform. The manufacturer then typically obtains launch orders for the product from the buyer. The company will develop the product in parallel with carrying out the research and development. In the case of an aircraft, there will be extensive testing to certify it with the airworthiness authorities. Eventually, the CoPS will start full-scale production.

For mass-market products such as iPhones, however, the product development comes first, then the production, and then the marketing to the end user. The interaction with the end customer tends to be at the back end of the process, though with CoPS, the relationship with the end user is often intimate and collaborative.

CoPS as a different type of product concept has been brought to the fore by the Science Policy Research Unit at the University of Sussex in England. With many of its researchers, the unit has published excellent material on this subject. In particular, the work of Keith Pavitt and Mike Hobday[4] has substantially aided the understanding of CoPS.

In terms of product characteristics, CoPS often have intricate component interfaces. The complexity comes from interrelating systems, and the consequences of the interactions can be hard to predict. CoPS have high unit costs, and tend to have small batch and low production numbers. For civil aircraft, for example, we are talking about 1,597 aircraft deliveries by Airbus and Boeing combined in 2015. If we go back to the ubiquitous iPhone, we are talking about 48 million units delivered in 2015. They are different concepts and constructs.

In terms of the innovation process, the interaction with a customer is deep with CoPS. A good example of this is the development of the Boeing 777.[5] The development of this aircraft was conducted by Boeing in close engagement with its airline customers. Customers had major input into the design specifications of the aircraft. This occurred even before any metal was cut for production of the aircraft.

With simpler products, the innovation process is focused with suppliers, on ensuring that the drumbeat of the supply chain is up and running, and on making sure that those operations are optimized and efficient. This is a logical priority if production levels are in the millions.

The innovation process for CoPS typically utilizes a high degree of people-embedded knowledge.[6] For civil aircraft, there are experts on various aspects of the systems, which could include aircraft electronics, how the aircraft flies in terms of lift and drag, wing design, and of course, engine design (which is both an art and science).

Even today, much of the knowledge of putting a product design together still resides in experiential knowledge within engineers' heads. This is less so for simpler products, for which the specifications of individual components of a product are well defined and their interaction is straightforward. Contrast this with the complicated interaction of an aircraft engine with an aircraft as the aircraft is taking off or descending. The understanding of much of those interactions is empirical in nature.

Now let us compare the market characteristics between CoPS and simple products. CoPS markets are typically dominated by a small number of companies. Inherent in highly capital-intensive CoPS is the need for a high market share to justify investment. Contrast this with simpler products, which have many buyers and many sellers, with the result that the market is usually highly fragmented.

Similar to market characteristics is the number of buying transactions. For large jet aircraft, probably 400 to 500 major airlines around the world buy aircraft. With some of the simpler products there are millions of customers. Thus, the market structures are really different.

The other thing that that is interesting about CoPS is that they are often in administered markets. By that, I mean that government regulation is involved. What immediately comes to mind for civil aircraft is the unescapable role of the Federal Aviation Authority (FAA) (and its European equivalent) in authorizing and certifying aircraft, which is an extremely important aspect of the industry. Civil aircraft have to be certified or they cannot be flown with fare-paying passengers aboard. The arbiter of a simpler product is the market. If a simple product fails in its purpose, it will not sell, because there will be no demand for it.

CoPS will be a recurring theme throughout the rest of the book. Here, I have provided a general impression of what I mean when I use the term.

CoPs are important. It is crucial to understand that they are different from other high-technology products. The reality is that they comprise a large proportion of exports from developed nations in terms of value, though in terms of units, they do not catch much attention.

CoPS do not capture the imagination of business academia probably because their innovation process is not straightforward and is, by definition complex. It is hard to disaggregate and analyze CoPS because there is so much interrelatedness between the mechanisms of innovation of their various components. It is unfortunate that they do not capture much attention, because CoPS form an important part of the manufacturing base in developed countries such as the United States, Germany, and Japan.

Now that we have examined the fascinating area of CoPS, we will consider the globalization of high technology. CoPS are the ultimate in high-technology goods. They are at the technological barrier, where governments want to control the dissemination of technologies. In this next section, we will consider the role of government in both enabling and constraining high-technology globalization.

Globalization Is Allowed to Happen

It is widely assumed that globalization is inevitable and "the world is flat," as postulated in Thomas Friedman's book of the same name.[7] The idea of the inevitability of globalization has almost become an accepted fact by virtue of its continued repetition by the media and pundits, but the reality is that it is not a foregone conclusion, certainly for high-technology goods. I will be drawing a lot here from my conversations over the years with a colleague at Rolls-Royce, Jeff Merrell, who is the company's Vice President, Strategic Export Control—Americas.[8] He puts forward a thesis that globalization in high technology is allowed to happen.

What really happens is that national governments control the flow of technology. Ever since the Cold War ended, the regulations governing what technologies can be shared between countries has been relaxed. In the West, the United States is the ultimate arbiter on such things and has relaxed the usage of technology around the world. The point to remember about these regulations is that they can easily be reapplied and can be made more stringent than they are today.

A good example of this is sanctions against Russia. At the time of this writing, Russia is under sanctions from the West for its relationship with Ukraine. Part of the sanctions being imposed by the West includes the stopping of technology flow to Russia. This means that for the Russian oil industry, the push to develop oil fields in the Arctic has slowed down because it was heavily reliant on Western technology. Furthermore, the fate of the Russian regional jet made by Sukhoi is in question. It has several Western companies' products on it and has been affected by economic sanctions on sales financing imposed by the West. That has resulted in much reduced economic viability of the aircraft. To improve the salability of the aircraft, Sukhoi has put efforts underway to indigenize the parts of the aircraft supplied by Western countries.

What we see is that groupings of largely Western governments agree on what high technology can or cannot be exported. There is particular concern about dual-use technologies, which are those developed in the civil sector that can easily be utilized in the defense arena. One such grouping is the Wassenaar Arrangement export-control regime. Such regimes place constraints on many aerospace-related technologies.

Export-technology controls are not a new thing. In Europe, they can be traced back to the year 779, when Charlemagne first banned the export of Frankish arms to the Slavs. China banned gunpowder exports around the year 1090. More recently, 1940 saw the US Export Control Act, which banned the supply of aircraft parts to Japan. Then, post-World War II, an organization was established to oversee and control technology exports from the United States and other North Atlantic Treaty Organization-related countries.

One has to ask why governments want to control this technology. Principally, the rationale is related to the defense sector. The United States does not want technology that it has funded to be used against it by an adversary. The country does not want to see its high-technology products integrated into another nation's products if that nation is not friendly to the United States.

The constraints are real. In recent times, companies have been fined for exporting goods to banned nations, even though sometimes, the companies' products have found their way into an adversary country's products through incompetence. More draconian is that the government can ban such companies from bidding for US government contracts. Ultimately, if maleficence is found, even individuals can be fined and go to jail for illegally exporting controlled technologies, so technology controls can be a real constraint on trade. Such controls are always there and are particularly pertinent to aerospace. The implication is that if a nation is not on good terms with the United States or other Western countries and aspires to develop a civil aircraft, that nation is at a disadvantage. If that nation wants to buy products from the West to install on aircraft it is developing indigenously, it likely will not receive current technology.

Chapter Summary

We have addressed in this chapter the idea of the technological barrier and the reality that countries have to change their approach towards innovation when they want to compete head-to-head with developed nations. Instead of copying to catch up, they have to innovate themselves, and that is not an easy transition to make.

CoPS are different from other high-technology products. They are important to economies because they are high-value goods. There is significant intellectual property embodied into these CoPS, and they create significant exports for the United States.

The approach to innovation is different for CoPS than for other products. There is a deep engagement with the eventual user of products to ensure that the design of the products is fit for purpose. For example, for aircraft, this engagement often takes place before any aircraft production has started. For the buyer, it is a matter of trust that the manufacturer will deliver the product as specified. Obviously, there are "get out of jail" clauses in purchase contracts, but buyers are still making a big commitment to buy products unseen, trusting the producer or innovator to deliver the specification.

Industry structure for CoPS is concentrated because of the high capital value and infrastructure required to develop such products. There is also heavy government oversight because the consequences of failure of these products can be acute. CoPS are different from the layperson's perception of high-technology products. CoPS products are inherently complex, which is especially true for aircraft. An aircraft is like a spaceship, in that it flies at very high altitudes, has to create its own breathable environment, and has to last twenty years. It is a remarkably robust and sophisticated product.

Finally in this chapter, we touched upon the issue of government control of high-technology exports. Such control is important in CoPS and pervades the civil aircraft industry. This is because aircraft technology is inextricably linked to the defense of countries; aerospace products are often used by defense and military, hence the risk.

Export-control regimes can be relaxed, but the notion that current Western aerospace technology can be exported to a potential adversary is not accurate. If a country aspires to have a leading-edge aircraft company, that country has to either be very friendly with the West or have the ability to develop its own leading-edge technology.

Comments on the Four Chapters about Foundational Concepts

In the first four chapters, I have laid the groundings that we will be referring to through the rest of the book. We have explored subjects at a fast pace, but I have provided readers with references to follow up on subjects if they wish to learn more.

As I stated in the introduction, one of the objectives of this book is to be accessible. This is why I have taken an approach of providing an overview of the foundational concepts with the idea of referring back to them later in the book. I have addressed some of the basic economic concepts, such as the three-sector model, comparative advantage, and entry barriers. I have explored the subject of innovation, industrial policy, and high-technology products. CoPS have been discussed at length.

Now that I have provided you with some of the underpinning, it is time to discuss the civil aircraft industry in more depth.

5.

The Civil Jet Aircraft Industry: An Overview

In the previous chapters, we looked at the foundational concepts of national industrial development and entry barriers. In the following chapters, we will integrate these concepts with an understanding of the civil aircraft market, but here, we start looking at the civil aircraft industry in more detail and drive forward toward the book's overall theme: Entry into civil aircraft manufacturing is hard. In this chapter, we will consider the complexity of an aircraft and some of the civil aircraft industry's basics. Then we will profile the incumbents and aspirants who want to enter the industry.

First, we need to remind ourselves of the scope of this book. Although we addressed this in the introduction, it is worth restating here: The scope of the book covers civil jet aircraft to transport fare-paying passengers—aircraft that are used to transport civil passengers from A to B, including airliners such as the ubiquitous Airbus A320 and the Boeing 737 product families—and regional jet aircraft. The reason for scope wider than simply civil jet aircraft is that most industry aspirants often start at the smaller end of aircraft size, and these smaller aircraft predominate in the regional jet sector.

It is tempting to consider defense aircraft markets, but those markets have a very different business model.[1] Additionally, for those of us interested in globalization of high technology, the defense sector holds less interest because the United States is so dominant in the leading-edge technologies of defense aircraft. For new defense entrants, the entry challenge is more about geopolitical positioning than head-to-head commercial competition. This is less interesting from a business perspective; hence the concentration on civil aircraft.

One characteristic of civil aircraft is that they are, as we saw in the Chapter 4, complex product systems, or CoPS. These products are very interesting to analyze because entry barriers to producing them are so high. Some companies have achieved entry, but many have failed, which is what we will be exploring over the next few chapters. The eventual aim is to develop a framework to guide us on the route to success and to provide a structure so we can judge the merits of various market-entry strategies.

One of the important aspects of an aircraft is the interconnectedness of its various systems. Let me start to explain it more in a practical way rather than a theoretical way, by looking at how an aircraft engine interacts with the aircraft itself.

We can imagine that a civil jet aircraft customer such as American Airlines, British Airways, or Japan Airlines want an aircraft that has a lower fuel usage. This requirement will often be the responsibility of the aircraft engine manufacturer to deliver. The aircraft engine manufacturer will consider how it could achieve this challenge and conclude it needs to makes changes within the innards of the engine. Particularly, say, in the back-end of the engine in a module called the turbine. This could involve the changing of the material of blades in the turbine which would enable it to handle higher temperatures. This will improve fuel efficiency. However, it will have a knock-on effect throughout the rest of the engine. For instance, this change in material might change the weight of the component itself, requiring redesign of the disc that carries the blades. It will require a re-matching of turbine flow capacities. It could also result in the turbine rotating at a higher speed. This will then have an impact at the front of an engine in a connected module called the compressor and may result in the need for a compressor redesign.

Another effect of changing the turbine material and increasing its temperature capability could be an increase in the thrust of the engine (i.e. the force that enables the aircraft to move forward). There are various mechanisms of capturing this improvement. The aircraft manufacturer could convert the benefit into increased aircraft range, or increase in the number of passengers that can be carried, or increase the speed of the aircraft. As can be seen, a simple change within the engine itself, like a material change of a component, can have implications that flow through to the critical performance measures of the aircraft.

Ultimately, when designing a new aircraft-and-engine combination, such improvements can be significant. If a new technology produces a substantially lower fuel usage, the aircraft manufacturer can trade the benefit in via improved carrying capacity, improved range, or faster speed, as we have seen, ultimately producing a smaller and lighter aircraft for a given mission requirement.

The interconnectedness of aircraft and engine is profound and is typical of many other systems in an aircraft, particularly where weight is concerned. Low aircraft weight is crucial, which is why a gas turbine is such a compelling power plant, as it is one of the most power-dense power generators available.

Another characteristic of civil aircraft is that they last a long time in operation, typically twenty years or more. As was alluded to in Chapter 4, they are flown in very harsh environments. The environment in which civil aircraft fly most of the time is deadly to people. Without being overly melodramatic, we can think of the aircraft like a spacecraft because if a person were outside of the aircraft, the person would not have long to live. In its twenty years of flying, the aircraft has to keep you safe at a high speed with a stunning degree of reliability and safety. To enable this, the product has to be at the technological barrier.

Civil Jet Aircraft Business Model

As one can imagine, the cost to develop an aircraft that performs in harsh environment is high. For a brand-new large civil aircraft, we are talking in terms of billions of dollars. With a new aircraft engine, $2 billion is a typical (R&D) cost. These are very large-scale investments.

As with other CoPS, the business model for civil aircraft is that the manufacturer will be developing the aircraft and taking initial orders at the same time, but the airframer will probably not formally launch the aircraft development until a minimum quantity of orders has been secured. This is to reduce financial risk for the aircraft manufacturer's owners and is typically mandated by the company board. So the aircraft manufacturer has to convince an airline that the manufacturer can deliver an aircraft—maybe in five years' time—to the specifications contractually agreed upon before the supply chain has even started cutting any metal. This is a risky business (colloquially termed the sporty game, after the title of the excellent book of the subject by John Newhouse). Initially, these aircraft will be sold at a discount from their gross price, and the manufacturer may not even break even on the first aircraft off the production line, but the aim is to lock in volume as soon as possible to move down the learning curve.

A feature of the civil aircraft industry, as in other CoPS industries, is that production rates are low. For instance, in 2014, Boeing produced only 724 aircraft. Early in aircraft production runs, the learning curve is very steep. There is therefore an imperative to obtain large and long production runs as soon as possible. This means gaining market share early is important for maximizing the financial profitability of the program.

The airframer sells to an airline or, in more recent years, to a financing company, which then leases the aircraft to an airline. Then, over the years, the profits from the sale of the aircraft will, they hope, pay for the R&D of the aircraft and ultimately provide an economic return to the company's shareholders.

The aircraft engine business has a slightly different business model. This is because there is a large aftermarket component to aircraft engines. Because they combust fuel, generate very high temperatures, and operate at high rotational speeds, engines tend to wear out. Engine parts deteriorate and therefore need replacing. This is not such an issue on the rest of the aircraft, which has a smaller aftermarket business.

For engines, which typically are about 15% of the aircraft's value, the business model is similarly to that of the aircraft. The engines will be sold at a heavy discount early on in the program to get product out into the marketplace. For the aircraft engine manufacturer, it is important to get the product out and flying so it generates spare parts and service revenue stream early on, with the aim of obtaining a return on R&D investment as soon as possible.

For larger aircraft, there is often the option to select engines from different manufacturers, which is something for an airline to consider. For smaller aircraft manufacturers the economics of the business case means that an engine choice for the aircraft is not worthwhile. For the aircraft manufacturer to go to the trouble of having the option is expensive. For larger programs it can make sense. In fact, sometimes, airlines demand that more than one engine supplier be available for a particular aircraft, so the engine manufacturer, on some occasions, will sell directly to the airline to gain many sales contracts.

The Participants in the Civil Aircraft Market

The field of participants (or incumbents) in today's civil aircraft market is small. We can count four companies that constitute the prime manufacturers of civil jet aircraft in the world. In this section, I provide a brief survey and description of each of these four companies, namely:

- Airbus

- Boeing

- Bombardier

- Embraer

Airbus

Airbus is a grouping that was created as a deliberate act of industrial policy by European governments. [2] In the 1970s, it became clear that individual nations' civil aircraft industries within Europe—in the United Kingdom, France, and Germany in particular—could not compete economically based solely on their home markets. The R&D cost had become too large for one nation's demand to cover, and it became clear that the old structure of separate national industries was not viable.

Because of this, the Europeans realized that they needed a much bigger participant in the industry to compete against the American companies Boeing and McDonnell Douglas. (McDonnell Douglas was later absorbed into Boeing.) Airbus was thus created by linking several countries' civil aircraft capabilities. We will look into the history of Airbus in more detail in the section of government-support rationales.

Airbus now provides competition with Boeing in every sector. It has the Airbus A320, which is a 150-seater that goes head-to-head against the Boeing 737. Airbus also has larger aircraft that compete with their Boeing equivalents—Airbus families such as the A330, A340, A350, and A380.

This latter aircraft is the largest civil aircraft in production in the world today.

Boeing

Most people have heard of Boeing. The company has a large defense business as well as other businesses, but when most people think of Boeing, they think of civil aircraft. Its civil aircraft business had sales on the order of $60 billion in 2014. To give you some idea of the scale of that, Google had $66 billion in sales in 2013. In the pharmaceutical business, Glaxo-SmithKline had sales of $37 billion. Boeing is a large company, but so is its civil aircraft business in its own right.

Boeing has been in the industry for a long time. It entered the civil jet aircraft market shortly after World War II. During the war, it developed military jet transport aircraft, but the end of the war obviated that need, so the company decided to convert the aircraft into a civil aircraft, which was ultimately transformed into the legendary four-engine Boeing 707, which entered service in 1957.

Over the years, the Boeing product portfolio has grown. New aircraft programs were added and older aircraft types terminated because of technological or economic obsolescence. The Boeing 707 and 727 died, for example, whereas the 737, which has been in production for over thirty years, has become one of the mainstays of the company. The Boeing 737 is a 150-seat class aircraft and carries much of the domestic load within the United States and other large markets in Europe and China. Other Boeing aircraft include the 787, which we will look at in a little more detail later, the 777, and the 747, which is still in production as of the writing of this book.

Boeing is the quintessential civil aircraft manufacturer. Clearly, it knows the industry well and has been very successful. It is answerable to shareholders, but it has a large defense business, which enables it, particularly as European companies would argue, to spin off technology funded by the Department of Defense to civil aircraft. This gets into the issue of subsidies, which we will address in a later chapter.

Bombardier

Bombardier is a Canadian company, and the creation of it as a civil aircraft business is interesting.[3] Bombardier is different from other incumbents because it was created via a company-acquisition strategy. The process started with the Bombardier's acquisition of a company called Canadair, which was a Canadian government-owned aircraft manufacturer. The business jet that the company produced ultimately provided Bombardier's regional jet family, the CRJ family. They also acquired Learjet, based in Wichita, in the United States, which produces small business jets. Then they bought de Havilland of Canada,[4] which is a turboprop aircraft manufacturer, finally they acquired Short Brothers of Belfast, in Northern Ireland. All of these companies were financially distressed at the time of purchase. Bombardier's strategy was to roll up those companies and create a coherent civil aircraft manufacturing entity. It has been successful at that.

The current looming question about Bombardier is about its move into larger civil jets that compete with the bottom end of Airbus's and Boeing's product lines. The company is developing a family of aircraft called the CSeries. At the time of writing the first member of the family is close to entering into service. The order book is not as the company would wish. There are some concerns about whether that program will provide a return on its investment and the Canadian government may provide financial support to the company.

An important aspect about the Canadian aerospace industry is that there is no defense sector to speak of in Canada. The aerospace industry is essentially all civil, but the government has designated aerospace as strategic (which we will consider later in the book). This means that the government is willing to provide heavy support for its indigenous civil aircraft business. That sometimes will put Canada at odds with countries that claim that they do not support their home industries as much as the Canadians support their own.

Worthy of note about Bombardier is that, despite being quoted on Montreal's stock exchange, it is managed or directed by a family. The

Beaudoin/Bombardier family still has majority voting rights for running the company, so it is a family-run business.

Embraer

Embraer is a Brazilian manufacturer and is now the third-largest civil aircraft manufacturer in the world. [5] In a similar way to Airbus, it was born of industrial policy, a deliberate act by the Brazilian government to create an aerospace industry, and it has been highly successful.[6] We will consider Embraer's entry and how it was successful, because it is a rare example of success and it is important to understand how it achieved its success so we can learn lessons for other potential new entrants.

Brazil had a deliberate policy of slow, incremental development for its national champion, Embraer, which now participates in the regional aircraft market, providing aircraft with 70–130 seats with its E-Jet range. Before that program was established, however, the company had developed a 50-seater jet aircraft family called the ERJ 145. Prior to that, it had a 30-seat turboprop aircraft, which had been preceded by a 19-seat turboprop, and yet before that, Embraer was manufacturing licensed-build and piston-powered very small aircraft for the US manufacturer Piper.

As you can see from the list of products, Embraer developed incrementally from small aircraft upward and has been successful in its entry. As of today, it not only participates in the regional aircraft market but also, over the past seven to eight years, has managed a successful entry into the business jet sector with its Legacy and Phenom product lines.

Aspirant companies/nations

Above was a quick overview of the incumbents in the civil aircraft industry. In addition to these four, several aspirant companies have aircraft in development that will potentially enter service in the coming years. These companies are Mitsubishi, China's COMAC, and Russia's Sukhoi. Brief profiles of these aspirants to the civil jet market follow.

Mitsubishi (of Japan)

Mitsubishi of Japan has been a participant in the industry since before World War II. Its heritage goes back to 1928. During the war, it produced a wide range of capable aircraft, including the famous Mitsubishi A6M ("Zero") fighter. As we will see when we look at Japanese industry efforts in more detail, the country was banned by the occupying forces from participating in the aerospace industry for seven years immediately after World War II, which stifled the Japanese industry's development.

In 1963, Mitsubishi reentered the civil aircraft industry with the development of the MU2 turboprop aircraft, followed by the Diamond business jet. Mitsubishi exited the business when it sold the rights to the Diamond to Beech in December 1985. (This aircraft went on to be renamed the Beech 400.)[7]

As a large civil aircraft subcontractor Mitsubishi has been a partner on many programs, particularly with Boeing and, to a lesser extent, Bombardier. This has enabled Mitsubishi to develop an expertise in manufacturing aircraft wings.

Mitsubishi is bringing a regional jet called the MRJ, the Mitsubishi Regional Jet, to the market. This aircraft is a 70–80-seater and first flew in November 2015. The program has orders but is running late, and there is a question whether the program will ultimately be successful financially.

It could be speculated that Mitsubishi has now realized how difficult it is to certify a civil aircraft—a lot more difficult than it looked from the perspective of a highly capable supplier of aircraft wings to Boeing and Bombardier. We will explore the challenge of converting from supplier to full-system integrator later.

COMAC (of China)

We will have a deeper examination of China's industry later.[8] For now, we content ourselves to know that the country's current foray into the civil aircraft industry is being spearheaded by the ARJ21 regional aircraft. This program, like Mitsubishi's MRJ, is also behind schedule. The ARJ21 adds to a long line of attempts by the nation to enter the civil jet aircraft market. It is yet to be seen whether COMAC will be successful in a global market sense with this particular aircraft. Meanwhile, however, the industry has started developing its next aircraft, the C919, which will compete with the Boeing 737 and Airbus A320 families.

Sukhoi (of Russia)

Russia's entrance into the market has actually taken place. The civil aircraft it has produced is called the Superjet, which has been built in engagement with European and Western suppliers such as Safran of France and Leonardo of Italy. The aircraft has flown and has been delivered to largely Russian airlines but has also seen some deliveries in the West to a Mexican airline.

At the time of writing, the momentum of Sukhoi's program has been severely hit by the sanctions against Russia as a consequence of its actions in the Ukraine. The most restrictive impact has been on sales financing support for aircraft. One of the lessons to be learned here is that if a company wishes to sell in the West, it has to accept the rules of West. This is a subject we will consider later.

Other Aspirant Nations

There are other countries that aspire to enter the industry but have not done so yet. These range from Korea[9] to Indonesia,[10] India,[11] Turkey,[12] and potentially Mexico.[13] Each has raised the prospect of attempting to create its own civil aircraft manufacturing industry. Indonesia did come close to establishing an industry via a company called Industri Pesawat Terbang Nusantara (IPTN), led by Dr. B. J. Habibie. The country was following an entry strategy similar to that of Embraer, but the 1997 Asian financial crisis put an end to government support for the effort.[14]

Engine Companies

Finally, while we are discussing the civil aircraft market, we need to consider the engine manufacturers. This is because they are important in terms of bringing an aircraft to fruition. The linkage and the interaction of the engine with civil aircraft are profound and important.

There are four civil jet engine manufacturers: General Electric,[15] Pratt & Whitney,[16] Rolls-Royce, and Safran (formerly known as Snecma). General Electric's entry into the jet business was just after World War II. This is when the initial prototypes of the jet engine were brought over from England and GE was selected by the US government to lead the jet engine revolution in the United States. The company later moved into the civil side of the industry with derivatives from the military engines.

Rolls-Royce's entry in the civil engine market was early in the last century, with piston engines. On the jet-engine side, they moved very quickly after World War II and powered the first civil jet aircraft, called the Comet. Rolls-Royce has been a constant presence in the industry in terms of powering civil aircraft.

Pratt & Whitney has also been in the industry for many years, and it has a subsidiary company called Pratt & Whitney Canada,[17] which makes small engines for the business jet and regional aircraft marketplaces.

Safran is the French aero engine company. It produces very small engines through its subsidiary Turbomeca. Safran has a major engine program called the CFM56, which is a 50-50 joint venture with GE. This engine powers the Boeing 737 and the Airbus A320 families.

Safran has always had aspirations to have its own strategy independent of GE. To pursue this ambition, it is bringing two new programs to the market. The first is the SaM146 engine, which has been developed with NPO Saturn of Russia and powers the Russian Superjet. Second is the Silvercrest engine, which will power large business jets.

Aircraft Engine People Leading Aircraft Companies

Before we draw this chapter to a close, I want to discuss the interesting phenomenon of senior engine managers moving to lead aircraft companies. One of the fascinating sub-stories of the aircraft industry is that of the interrelationship of engine companies and airframe manufacturers. Often, we see this at very senior levels. In recent times, we have seen several engine manufacturer leaders go on to senior positions at aircraft manufacturers. It is quite interesting. The reverse move, of an aircraft manager leading an engine company occurs less often.

For instance, at Boeing, we see James McNerney, who is their retiring CEO at the writing of this book. He ran GE's aircraft engine business from 1997 to 2000. At Airbus a few years ago, Louis Gallois was CEO, but earlier in his career, he was CEO of Snecma (now Safran). Alain Belle-mare, a retired Pratt & Whitney executive, now leads Bombardier. Another example is Scott Ernest, CEO of Textron Aviation (Cessna); prior to that role, he was a GE engines manager for 29 years.

It is an interesting aspect of the industry to see the connectedness not only at the technological and product level but also at the personnel level. We often see it also in the business jet industry, with executives moving from business jet manufacturer to business jet manufacturer; this seems to be part of the dynamic of the industry.

Chapter Summary

In this chapter, we have gone into a little more depth about CoPS and have looked at both the civil aircraft and aircraft engine business models, in addition to some background of each of the major aircraft manufactur-ers, to gain some context for the aircraft industry. This is required so that when we talk about entry barriers, we can use industry examples and anecdotes, to enable us to start with at least a little bit of knowledge about these companies.

Chapter 6 will be addressing entry barriers. We have addressed them in a theoretical sense already, but now we are going to make a connection between theory and practice with the specifics of the civil aircraft industry.

6.

Entry Barriers and Civil Aircraft

In this chapter, the theoretical concepts explored earlier in the book are used to explain the business realities of the civil aircraft industry. The starting place of our analysis will be based on Bain's framework of entry barriers.[1] He proposed three generic barriers to entry: product differentiation, absolute cost advantage, and scale economics. Each will be examined here with regard to their relevance to the civil aircraft industry.

Product Differentiation

In the case of product differentiation, the role of the user is important. With this form of entry barrier, there is consumer goodwill towards the incumbents—the aircraft manufacturers in the case of the civil aircraft industry. Although most of the economic literature tends to focus on the role of advertising on consumer goodwill, this is not important in the case of civil aircraft. Buyers of civil aircraft are sophisticated, intelligent buyers of the product and are rarely swayed by advertising claims.

The first main product-differentiation feature of the civil aircraft industry is the high level of sunk costs that the airlines have invested in understanding the existing airframer's products. Most airlines have an aircraft engineering department that is expected to keep up to date with the developments of each airframer's offering. This learning process may even take the form of the engineering department being involved intimately in the development of a new civil aircraft as advisors to the manufacturer. When an airline is about to purchase a new aircraft, this department will be called upon to advise on the best product offering for the airline's particular route structure. Creating and maintaining this knowledge base only about the incumbent airframers offerings is expensive. The expense of having to understand a new entrant's product will not be welcomed by the airlines unless the new entrant offers substantial benefits over the incumbents. Indeed, an airline may be satisfied that there are only two aircraft offerings because this will create enough of the competition that they would like to see. Airlines, as sophisticated customers, recognize that there is an economic question regarding how many airframers can be supported by the market. Consequently, some airlines may need convincing that the threat of entry from a new competitor is really in the long-term best interests of the industry. Alternatively, some airlines recognize that they have a role in shaping the structure of the aircraft industry and see it in their best interest to reduce duopoly or monopoly economic power. All these considerations need to be analyzed by the airline and overcome by the new entrant.

The second product-differentiation entry barrier that will have to be overcome is that of reputation. The incumbents have a track record of delivering products that meet the consumers' specifications and are delivered on time. They have shown that when they have encountered technical problems, they have the know-how and resources to solve those problems. This type of preference for incumbents is significant for airlines. An airline needs a product that meets its specifications because it will almost certainly compete with an airline that has a different aircraft that meets its own specifications. The airframer's reputation for delivering a product to specification is therefore an important entry barrier.

Absolute Cost Advantage

Absolute cost advantages arise for incumbents when they have preferred access to superior resources over new entrants. There are six main areas in which the aircraft manufacturer has significant absolute cost advantages: patents, learning and experience, legislative restrictions, subsidies, sunk costs, and the higher cost of financing for aspirants.

Patents

The economic literature tends to focus on patents as a cost advantage, which is probably because these are relatively easy to quantify and therefore analyze. Unlike in the pharmaceutical industry, patent protection of technology industry until recently has not been a significant barrier to entry to the civil aircraft industry. Patenting activity does take place in the civil aircraft industry, but competition takes place at a level of total system integration (i.e., the aircraft itself). Although a patent can confer advantage at the component level, technological superiority for a patented component is often offset by a weakness elsewhere in the aircraft. This perspective may be changing, however. A recent example of this change was the recent patent fight in the aero-engine industry over swept fan blade technology. This was a legal battle between Rolls-Royce and Pratt & Whitney, where initially Rolls-Royce developed a forward swept fan design that produced a substantial efficiency gain, and conferred a potentially significant competitive advantage. In response Pratt & Whitney sought to mimic the innovation across a large number of its engine models while at the same time challenging the validity of the Rolls-Royce patent. When the Pratt & Whitney challenge to the Rolls-Royce patent failed, Rolls-Royce accused Pratt & Whitney of infringement on a massive scale. This law suit could have resulted in an injunction prohibiting further use and damages of several billion dollars. As often found with legal battles, the other party countersues, and this was the case here. Pratt & Whitney countersued, accusing Rolls-Royce of copying a patented Pratt & Whitney fan design and asked the U.S. International Trade Commission to ban the importation of infringing Rolls-Royce engines to the US. Consequently, each manufacturer faced the prospect that it would be unable to deliver engines to its airframe customers, Airbus and Boeing, an unthinkable situation. Not surprisingly, after some initial skirmishes in the Court and at the ITC, the dispute was eventually resolved out of court by a commercial settlement involving a cross-licensing of technology.[2]

This episode shows how patents have become more important than they used to be in the industry. Now every piece of technology and every incremental innovation has become important to competitiveness.

Learning and Experience

As described in Chapter 4, airframers have accrued substantial tacit knowledge of the design, development, and manufacture of civil aircraft. They are uniquely positioned as system integrators to understand the interaction between all the various subsystems of an aircraft. They have not only an intimate technical understanding of current civil aircraft but also the program-management capabilities to optimize their networks between the airlines, regulators, partners, and subcontractors. This is a formidable entry barrier. Even highly capable suppliers can obtain only a restricted understanding of the totality of the development of a civil aircraft, because they have only limited access to the networks of customers, regulators, and suppliers.

In addition, incumbents, by virtue of their past successes, get better at making aircraft because they have done it many times before. Manufacturing engineers term this the learning curve effect. An incumbent can move down learning curves for a new aircraft more quickly than new entrants can.[3] A new entrant has less experience than an incumbent, and that means the new entrant inherently has higher costs. Boeing, Airbus, Embraer, and Bombardier have a lot of experience in the manufacturing process and have built many thousands of aircraft each. A new entrant does not have this experience and has significant learning to do just to put together its first aircraft.

Legislative Restrictions

The issue of legal restrictions as an entry barrier is controversial. Aircraft manufacturers have to pass rules, regulations, and tests set by the relevant certification authorities before they can supply passenger-carrying aircraft. The two most important authorities are the US Federal Aviation Authority (FAA) and the European Aviation Safety Agency (EASA). No aircraft in the United States or Europe can fly without the aircraft and engine being certified by these authorities. Because the FAA and EASA do not develop aircraft themselves, they have to rely on the current airframers to advise them on whether new regulations are feasible. This relationship from a new entrant's point of view is somewhat worrying because the incumbent is advising the regulatory authority. In this situation, it is unlikely that a new entrant could put forward a radically new design concept because the regulatory authority will seek advice from the incumbents on the concept's feasibility and the nature of this advice is likely to serve the incumbents' self-interest. From a new entrant's perspective, this could be seen as favoring the existing aircraft manufacturers.

Subsidies and Government Support

The important role of subsidies in the civil aircraft industry will be addressed in the next chapter, but I will introduce the subject here. Every company in the civil aircraft industry receives either direct (project-related) or indirect (technology-proving) state support. As was described earlier in this book, the rationales for this support range from capital market-failure arguments and technology-diffusion benefits to astute lobbying to justify job protection aid. The most important question regarding these subsidies in the context of this book is not whether subsidies are fair but rather whether they provide the airframer with an advantage over a new entrant. The answer to this question is yes, in two respects. First, much of the tacit knowledge built up by the airframer has been paid for by subsidies that have gone on for many years. A new entrant will have a high investment to fund the effort to replicate this knowledge. Second, the absolute size of the incumbents will be larger than any potential new entrant. The level of subsidy that can be spent by the existing airframer therefore is more than the new entrant will be able to spend. Essentially, the amount a company can receive in subsidies is related somewhat to its size, meaning a new entrant is naturally disadvantaged.

Each country has its own mechanism for supporting its aerospace industry, but the case of the United States is special. The United States has a policy for the aerospace industry, unlike the automobile, consumer electronics, and machine tool industries. This takes the form of indirect aid channeled through the Department of Defense and NASA grants. The touchstone of American strategic foreign policy is to force projection over global distances with technological superiority. When cascaded down to specific product requirements, this naturally leads to the need for advanced fighter jets and long-range transport aircraft—hence the need to actively create and sustain a world-class aerospace industry. The technologies developed for these military aircraft are often spun off into the civil industry.

Other nations have special industrial policies for aerospace. What makes the United States different is the commitment to continue its world leadership and the high level of funding expended by the government to support this aim. A new entrant targeting the civil aircraft industry will therefore enter an industry in which "America, Inc." has an industrial policy. This may be the ultimate market entry barrier, particularly for countries that look to the United States for their defense (see Chapter 8).

Other nations have financial support regimes. Europe, for instance, has a set of mechanisms to support Airbus. The most important of these took the form of direct, repayable financial support to the airframer operations in each of the nations where Airbus operates. It was a complicated structure. Each nation was allocated a workshare on an aircraft. Then this workshare received support from the home government (i.e., Germany, France, or the United Kingdom). In the case of the United Kingdom, this support was for an aircraft wing designed by Airbus at its two facilities within that country. The support would then be paid back via some form of royalty-type arrangement. Canada has a similar regime to support its indigenous airframe manufacturer, Bombardier, while Brazil has a similar regime to support Embraer.

Sunk Costs

With sunk costs, incumbents have a large infrastructure that they can draw upon to support their programs, which have often existed for decades. Even the newest entrant to the marketplace, Embraer of Brazil, has a large infrastructure that it has developed over decades. It consists of a collection of test beds, engineering facilities, and the tacit experience inside the engineers' brains, which has all been paid for. All the engineers have been trained over many programs. Much of the capital expenditure on test beds will probably be paid off and is a sunk cost, so there is no cost for them on the balance sheet of these companies, but a new entrant has to incur these costs all at once to participate. This is one of the entry costs of getting into the business.

Higher Finance Costs for Aspirants

A new entrant, by definition, has zero or very little track record. An organization financing a new entrant has to charge an inherent risk premium for the high risk of failure in a new entrant compared to an incumbent. This is another absolute cost advantage that the incumbents have and is yet another burden for a new entrant to overcome, which is why all new entrants into civil aircraft manufacturing have financial backing from their home governments.

Scale Economics

One of the economies-of-scale entry barriers is a characteristic called the percentage effect. The percentage effect depends on the size of the minimum efficient level of production relative to the industry's total capacity. It is particularly relevant when the efficient scale is a substantial proportion of the total industry size (i.e., an oligopoly market structure). In an oligopoly industry structure, such as aircraft manufacturing, if an entrant decides to enter the market at an efficient scale, the move is likely to reduce prices (i.e., classic supply-and-demand economics). Although an incumbent can absorb such a price reduction, the reduction will be more detrimental to a new entrant's economic rationale for entering the industry. The new entrant has to assume that prevailing market prices prior to its entry will reduce when it enters the market. This is above and beyond any discounting that the new entrant needs to deploy to garner market share quickly.

Another aspect of scale economics to consider is that a participant must have a minimum share of the market for its participation to be economical. The reason is that each company has a huge infrastructure, a large capital inventory, and a large cadre of engineers to pay and to keep knowledgeable. To pay for this, a company has to achieve a minimum of market share. It is difficult to decide what that is, but one can easily imagine that an incumbent with zero market share has a challenging task because it is bearing the full costs of participation with all the disadvantages of coming late to the marketplace. It will initially have no sales revenue, so it has to carry the large capital investment in new test beds and facilities, engineer training, and product development, whereas the incumbents have cash flows coming in from prior products.

Another type of economies-of-scale barrier is risk premium here for investment. We discussed risk premia as an absolute cost advantage earlier in this chapter, but there is also an economy-scale advantage for incumbents that is related to financial risk. Investment required for new aircraft development is typically billions of dollars. Companies such as Boeing and Airbus, because they are so large, are seen as lower risks to fund at such levels than are new entrants, so there is a double risk-premium effect. First is the risk premium because of inexperience, which is an absolute cost disadvantage. Then is the sheer scale issue, in which a small company entering against a big company is seen as risky. This is a scale-economies risk.

Chapter Summary

This chapter has considered entry barriers and how they apply to the civil aircraft manufacturing industry. I think we can conclude that the entry barriers to civil aircraft manufacturing are formidable. The technical and financial barriers to entry are large, so it is hardly surprising that governments get involved. We will return to the subject of entry barriers in Chapter 8, but a good understanding of the role of government is useful before proceeding, so in the next chapter, we will look at the role of government in the civil aircraft industry.

7.

Government and Civil Aircraft Manufacturing

In this chapter, we will consider the important role of government inter-vention into the civil aircraft sector. To do this adequately, we widen the subject area to include the defense industry because often, the initial gov-ernment involvement in the aircraft sector is for defense rather than com-mercial industrial policy reasons.

As explained earlier, government industrial policies are usually justified on the grounds of what economists call market failure. "Industrial policy" is an umbrella term for a range of government programs that are used to cor-rect market failure. These include competitive, regional, trade, and inno-vation policies. Although there are many government-support mechanisms for the civil aircraft industry, the most important type of intervention is financial support for research and development (R&D).

Economists argue that for some company R&D investments the firm car-rying out the R&D often does not capture all the resulting financial ben-efits. Because of this an adequate financial return cannot be achieved for the firm's owners and some good projects "fail" to take place as a result. To correct this market failure, an outside agency (i.e., the government) has to intervene. This justification for government action tends to be applied to research rather than closer to product development. The controversy regarding this rationale is less about its intellectual rigor from an econo-mist's point of view and more about where the line is drawn between research and close-to-market product development. In other words, at what point does correcting market failure become market distortion?

The aerospace industry is one sector where the debate about government intervention is particularly vociferous. The extent of state intervention is often justified with the explanation that aerospace is special. To analyze some of these issues, this chapter examines differing government approaches regarding support of civil aircraft industry development.

First, the chapter revisits the reasons why governments intervene in the high-technology sector as initially described in Chapter 3. This duplicated (but reduced) overview is included for the reader who missed this background by skipping the earlier chapters on theoretical concepts. Then the chapter reviews government intervention for individual country or regional units: the United States, Europe, Brazil, Canada, Japan, China, and Russia. The final section of the chapter then examines the differences and similarities of state-support justifications and discusses the implications of the findings, with the aim of seeing how these justifications differ from country to country and classifying common themes between developing and developed nations.

Why Governments Support High-Technology Industries

Seven justifications for state support for high-technology sectors are briefly reviewed below. Some of the justifications are supported by accepted economic theories, and others are political.

Public Good, Defense of the Nation

If left to the market, the defense of a nation would be inadequate (i.e., the market fails), and as a result, the government will always intervene in this area. For example, if a nation perceives itself significantly threatened by outside forces, the reaction is often the development of home grown high-technology capabilities. The drive for a domestic high-technology industry is the desire for self-sufficiency. Many technological innovations have been created from a nation's need to match an adversary's capability. The national-defense rationale has often led to the establishment of whole industries (including aircraft manufacturing).

Capital Market Failure

The existence of government financial support to the aerospace sector for aircraft development implies that the government accepts the existence of capital market failure. The usual sources of funding available to firms for investment (equity and debt markets) charge excessively high rates of return on R&D programs with long payback periods typical of aircraft projects. The high rates charged to the development programs lower the programs' internal rate of return, so the programs may not achieve the firms' cost of capital. A program would not proceed under these circumstances. Capital market failure inhibits innovation in several ways but is the result of differing perspectives of risk, incentives, and asymmetric information.

Technology Diffusion

The spread of use of new technology is known as technological diffusion. The diffusion of technology is of central concern to anyone interested in the linkage between innovation and economic progress; as a result, the subject has been researched extensively.[1] A government's aim in encouraging technology diffusion is to distribute knowledge widely within the country and thereby lift the nation's overall capability. The spin-offs can be in the form of new technologies used by other industries and the transfer of skilled people from high technology into lower-technology sectors. Government funding is given to companies knowing that the companies do not capture all the economic benefit of the investment but that the economy as a whole benefits (i.e., social returns are greater than private returns). As the aerospace industry is a high-technology industry, it provides significant benefits to the economy. Much of the technologies resulting from the aerospace industry will be diffused into the economy via transfer to other industrial users.

If technology diffusion is the aim of an industrial policy, the implication is that many indigenous companies should participate and share results from government-funded activities. This policy stance is opposite to the one in which the country wants to create a "national champion" that can compete with international incumbents in the industry. Often, within nations, individual firms aspire to become national champions while the government's objective is to improve technology diffusion, but these aims are incompatible.

Industry Targeting

The notion of industry targeting first gained prominence with the success of the Japanese economy after the Second World War. The thinking behind this approach is that scarce government funds are targeted at specific industries. Furthermore, an element of protectionism for domestic manufacturers is often involved. The government's agenda is to progressively move the country's innovation center of gravity from low-technology to high-technology industries. In essence, the government is attempting to change the nation's comparative advantage. Industry targeting is therefore popular in developing countries but less so in developed nations.

Strategic Trade Theory

Strategic trade theory is a relatively new model and is controversial. The argument for government support here is based on the assertion that the market for a product is dominated by one nation and funding to support the establishment of another competitor will create beneficial competition. This competition will then reduce monopoly profits and produce a net increase in economic welfare. The controversy centers on whether there is an overall improvement to the world economy if the subsidy required to set up the new entrant is included in the calculation.

Job Protection/Creation

High-technology industries require highly paid researchers, engineers, and managers. Their wages, when spent in the local economy, create and support more jobs and thereby grow the economy as a whole. Neoclassical economists argue that this justification is weak, however, because without the government support, the work would go to the most efficient source. Investment to protect or create jobs is therefore seen as wasteful and "distorting"; however, most governments do not take an altruistic view of the world and seek to maximize their national interest. Job creation is therefore a factor that governments consider when judging whether they will support an industry, particularly when the decision making is highly politicized.

Leveling the Playing Field

In this case, the government is lobbied by the domestic industry, which argues that it is unfairly treated when compared to the support its competitors receive in other countries. The (alleged) distorting actions of the competitors mean lower growth for the indigenous company and hence the country as a whole loses out. Domestically, the argument is often coupled powerfully with the rationale of job protection/creation rationale. The decision about to whether funding is made available is ultimately a political one.

Export Sales Financing

Before we move on to reviewing individual countries, we should discuss the role of export sales financing. This is yet another mechanism provided by governments to support their civil aircraft industries. When an aircraft manufacturer wants to sell to a foreign airline with a weak credit rating, the manufacturer's government will be called upon to guarantee the repayment of any loan. For the United States, this loan guarantee is provided by a government agency called EXIM (Export-Import) Bank. This support usually comes after the decision has been made to enter the industry, and the sales support mechanism does not engage until the aircraft are being delivered. Because the availability of export sales support is typically not a major consideration when making the strategic decision to enter the civil aircraft industry we will not consider it further in this book.

The civil aircraft industries receive government funding in most countries, but the justification for support differs widely. In the next section, specific examples of state support for civil aircraft industries are analyzed. The eight nations examined below were chosen because each exhibits specific facets of a particular state-support rationale and because sufficient evidence exists for assessing the success of support regimes.

Country Reviews

The United States

As stated early in this chapter, the defense justification for government intervention in the aerospace industry is important, nowhere more than in the United States, a superpower that operates its military on a global scale.[2] It therefore needs to have an advanced domestic aerospace industry to ensure that its strategic mission can be deployed successfully. The funding of this industry to support the nation's military stance provided the opportunity for technology spin-offs that enabled the start of the country's competitive civil aircraft industry.

There are two major funding sources of the aerospace industry in the United States: the Department of Defense (DOD) and NASA. The DOD provides considerable funding for new aeronautical endeavors,[3] in the form of grants, which is not required to be repaid. Furthermore, the company receiving the funding, to a large extent can use much of this technology in other sectors. For the most part, we can consider that many US aerospace companies entered the civil sector by developing military products and then spinning them off into the civil sector. This is really an important determinant of the United States' competitive advantage. The scale of DOD support is large, dwarfing anything similar in other nations, even large defense-oriented nations such as China and Russia.

When most people think about NASA, they think about the space program, but a proportion of its budget is allocated to civil aircraft programs. In recent years, these programs have concentrated on reduction of aircraft noise and emissions. Again, this funding takes the shape of a grant paid to the company to develop technology with no requirement for repayment. The contractor ends up having the technology.

The difference between NASA and the DoD is that NASA has as one of its missions the role of disseminating or diffusing technology to the rest of the industrial base, though that is not a prime mission of DOD funding. When companies apply for NASA-funded programs, they are aware that the technology is not ring-fenced for them alone and that it can be shared with other companies, and that is one issue they take into consideration.

Why have we discussed the defense aspect of US financial support mechanisms? Such discussion is required because of the extent of the spin-off into civil aircraft manufacturing, particularly in the early days of the industry. A lot of the competitive positioning of US aircraft companies can be traced back to the country's strategic imperative to project power over very long distances, and this required a leading aerospace capability.

Europe

There are two key issues about government support of aerospace within Europe. One is that, unlike the United States, Europe looks only its own geographic region in a political power sense. Secondly, the US provides a defense umbrella and is a guarantor of Europe's security. Because of this, the need to have a large defense industrial base is not as compelling in Europe as it is in the United States. This means that having technologies spun off from the military aerospace industry to the civil is not so prevalent. In addition, the defense industry in Europe is smaller than in the United States, so there is less opportunity to spin off into civil aircraft.

Another aspect in Europe is the acceptance of fostering high-wage high-technology jobs as a part of industrial policy. This is more politically acceptable in Europe than in the United States. The idea that government policy supports an industry because the industry generates high-wage engineering and high-skilled jobs is acceptable in many European nations, particularly Germany and France. This is because they highly value the manufacturing industry's contribution to their national economies.

The current civil aircraft industry within Europe centers on Airbus. Airbus was originally a government concept. It was conceived in response to the problem of the aerospace industries of individual European countries were not competitive with that of the United States. An example of this can be seen in the UK experience with several civil aircraft programs in the 1960s and 1970s. These included the Trident, VC10, and BAC One-Eleven aircraft, which were designed for home airlines such as the British Overseas Airways Corporation (BOAC) and British European Airways (BEA). All these aircraft failed economically.

European aircraft manufacturers tended to design aircraft for domestic airlines. As the aircraft were optimized for the domestic airlines they did not achieve export sales success. They were financially unsuccessful because they were not globally competitive. Even in those days, large R&D costs meant export sales in the global market were essential for financial success.

This situation was made more complicated because airlines were government-owned and were obligated to buy aircraft from home producers.

This is described in Martin Staniland's well-researched book *Government Birds: Air Transport and the State in Western Europe*:

> Some executives agreed: for example, the then chairman of BOAC, Sir Gerard ("Pops") d'Erlanger, confided to his successor that he had "never believed that it was the Corporation's job to make profits. The Corporation was there to support the British aircraft industry, to develop routes round the world, and so on."[4]

By the late 1960s, individual European national civil aircraft industries were failing and were about to exit the industry. It became apparent that to save them, nations would have to make some compromises. The solution was to create a pan-European company, which eventually became Airbus. The rumps of the civil aircraft industries within the various nations could be saved by creating a single company that would compete on a global scale.

The other context for the creation of Airbus was that there was a fear that Europe would not have a competitor to Boeing. The concern was that European airlines would be overcharged for American-built aircraft, effectively paying monopoly profits to US suppliers, which would ultimately be to the detriment of European consumers..

These reasons provided the justification that led governments to create and fund Airbus, the justification being that the overall wealth of Europe is enhanced by saving high-wage jobs and having technology spin-off effects within each nation. It also kept competition going in civil aircraft markets so the prices that European airlines paid would be lower (i.e., strategic trade theory).

Though Airbus is a pan-European concept, the funding mechanism is at the national level; each nation provides direct repayable program support. This is unlike the system in the United States. Boeing programs, such as that of the 787, do not receive direct support from the US government, but in Europe, the various elements manufactured within in Germany, for instance, are partially supported by the German government. Similarly, the wings and the aircraft assembly are supported by the UK and French governments, respectively.

We can see that there is a significant difference just by looking at these two approaches to government-support rationales. The US model provides no direct support for civil aircraft (except for some long-term technology funding through NASA). The technologies are generated in the burgeoning defense sector and are then spun off into the civil sector. In Europe, because there is not a large defense sector, the need is to create and sustain a civil aircraft manufacturing industry in which individual aircraft programs are funded directly.

As one can imagine, there have been tensions between the United States and Europe in terms of government support, and there have been several complaints to the World Trade Organization (WTO) by both sides.[5]

Today, there is a respite in the trade conflict between the two countries and a trade war has been averted, but the rhetoric can still get elevated. A written agreement that limits the US defense R&D funding as a percent of sales has lasted for several decades. That is their constraint, whereas in Europe, the constraint is that the level of direct repayable funding to programs is limited to around 30%.

Brazil

Brazil and its national champion, Embraer, provide a classic case study of how to successfully enter the civil aircraft industry.[6] Initially, the Brazilian government intended to create an aircraft company for local defense reasons. The company has morphed into its current highly successful form because the government adopted a national-champion funding approach.

The Brazilian aerospace strategy was to protect Embraer in its early stage as a government-owned entity until it achieved a critical mass. No other domestic manufacturer was allowed, so scarce funding was targeted at this one company. Eventually, Embraer became a publicly quoted company and remains the only aircraft company in Brazil. It continues to receive support from its home government, and that support includes finance support for aircraft sales outside of Brazil.

Canada

Canada's aircraft industry has been consolidated into one company called Bombardier, but the company has a long heritage that goes back to the British companies de Havilland and Canadair (formerly Canadian Vickers). Both were UK subsidiaries in Canada manufacturing aircraft for the local market. These local companies, through several changes of ownership, were consolidated into Bombardier, which constitutes the only civil aircraft manufacturer in Canada.

Even more so than Europe, Canada has a small defense business. It is similarly defended by the United States in terms of any grand strategic threat (the basis of this was laid down in the Ogdensburg Agreement, signed in 1940) and therefore has no need of a large defense industry. The country does, however, have a civil aircraft industry that employs high-wage engineers and generates technology and economic spin-offs. In a similar way to Europe, Canada views the civil aircraft industry as worth nurturing. Canada is perhaps the most clear-cut in stating that this aircraft industry is strategic for the country.[7] As such, it supports the industry vigorously, with significant funding: "As we well know, [in the aerospace sector] Canada is among the best in the world and it is the government's intention to maintain the structures and policies that will see it continue," Prime Minister Paul Martin, said in the House of Commons on November 18, 2004.

The Canadian mechanisms for support have changed over the years. They have moved from direct program support in a guise similar to the support in Europe, to funding generic technology. This generic technology eventually finds its way into near-market aircraft-development programs.

The scale of Canadian-government funding is at a similar level to Europe's: Typically, 30% of an R&D program is funded by the government. The other nuance in Canada is the importance of the local provinces in which the industry's factories are found, particularly Quebec.[8] They provide support as well, so the industry has a mixture of funding sources.

As in Europe, this form of support is attractive to a company because it is not considered a loan and thus does not appear on the company's balance sheet. The repayment mechanism is such that repayment is waived during the early production of the aircraft. Then after a certain number of aircraft have been delivered, a royalty on each one helps pay back the support from the government.

The program is controversial in Canada, and various organizations object to what they call corporate welfare, but both sides of the government complexion continue to support this funding mechanism because, as I said earlier, Canada's civil aircraft industry is seen as important for the nation as a whole. The funding mechanism is therefore likely to continue.

An interesting digression about the Canadian support mechanism illuminates the fear that aerospace programs could be lost from the nation. This fear was crystalized in the 1970s, when engine manufacturer Pratt & Whitney Canada had a labor dispute with its union employees.[9] The dispute resulted in the parent company in the United States transferring an aircraft engine program (the JT15) from Canada to the United States during the strike. This move broke the strike. From the Canadian government's point of view, this was alarming, because it showed that aerospace programs could leave the country a lot more easily than they had thought. This is one of the other reasons why the Canadian government is supportive of a company like Bombardier, which not only has facilities in Canada but also has the opportunity to put work into its facilities in the United States and Northern Ireland. Bombardier does have options, and this will be in the back of the mind of the Canadian government even though the company has strong roots in the country. This is another reason why Canadian government support is so beneficial.

Similar to the United States and Europe, Brazil and Canada share some tension over government support. Airbus and Boeing manufacture large airliners and compete directly; similarly, Embraer and Bombardier manufacture regional jets and business jets, and they are direct competitors. There has been conflict about government subsidies between both of these countries. The WTO findings have been related to aircraft sales finance. The Brazilian Pro-X program and the Canadian Crown corporation support for exports have been found to be illegal under the WTO rules. These programs have been changed to bring them into line with WTO guidelines. Both Embraer and Bombardier do receive support, and one can say that both companies are national champions.

Japan

As with other countries, Japan has the US defense umbrella (from the Treaty of Mutual Cooperation and Security, 1952) and until recently has been reticent about developing its own substantive defense capability. Another issue that is important about the Japanese context is that just after World War II, the country was banned from participating in the aerospace industry for five years. As it transpired, this was an important factor in Japan's lag in participation in the civil aircraft sector. Those five years were very important times of technological development, particularly because of the development of the gas turbine engine and the transition from piston-powered aircraft to jet aircraft, and Japan did not participate in the industry at this crucial time.

If we consider the government ethos of Japan in terms of its support for civil aircraft and other industries, we see that the government has targeted industries rather than companies. The industries have broad-based support mechanisms, and the heart of Japanese thinking is that technology diffusion is a priority because it brings up the nation as a whole.[10] Japan has no notion of funding a singular national champion.

The first Japanese attempt at entry into the civil aircraft industry came in the 1960s with the Nihon Aircraft Manufacturing Corporation (NAMC) YS-11 aircraft. This indigenous aircraft company had a disparate industrial structure with many companies participating, which enabled wide technology diffusion.

The more recent program partnership approach (with Boeing) has been directed by the Japanese government to include multiple domestic companies. This implies that the government is encouraging technology diffusion and is not aiming to create a national champion. This is an interesting contrast from the approach taken by Brazil and Canada.

In Japan, the types of funding mechanisms are similar to those of Europe and Canada. They tend to be direct-program-related funding mechanisms with repayment schemes, but very often, the constraint attached to the government's funding stream is that there should be many Japanese partners involved in the program. This subtle but important difference is significant if a country aims to create an indigenous aircraft manufacturer that can compete on a world scale. A technology-diffusion policy is not as effective as one that channels government resources into one national champion.

China

China is on everybody's mind at the moment because of its fast encroachment into various manufacturing sectors. There is a question about its government's aims for aerospace. Strategically, we can think of China as the only nation that has ambitions on a scale similar to that of the United States. It is easy to conclude that China has aspirations to ultimately become a global power.[11] To achieve this it is embarking on a strategy to develop its aircraft industry. The government support mechanisms are opaque, to say the least, but China seems to develop aircraft programs for what I call industrial policy reasons. The aim of these civil aircraft programs is to "learn by doing" and to generate the country's own technology. Competing in global markets is not the principal objective.

In a later chapter, we will dig deeper into China's track record of attempting entry into the civil aircraft industry, which goes back decades. So far, it is a record of failure, but the Chinese government's intent remains to support its industry, and it will take a long-term view. Whether it will be successful in competing on a global scale is not known, but many people fear it is imminent. One of the conclusions we will get to is that China's successful competition in this regard is perhaps further in the future than most people realize.

With China, there are a lot of interconnected themes: There is the defense imperative to be a global power. There is the view that civil aerospace is the next industry to conquer along the product added-value hierarchy, that it is just another industry to master on the route to becoming a developed nation. This could be seen as following the progression as described in the three-sector model covered in Chapter 2. As we have seen throughout this book, entry into civil aircraft is hard. The idea of moving up the technology hierarchy and creating high-wage jobs is imperative to China because the nation's historical competitive advantage of low manufacturing wages has been eroded. China simply needs to move up the technology value chain. The big question is whether it can achieve this.

Russia

Russia has a long history of manufacturing civil aircraft. After World War II, it created an industry that manufactured large quantities of civil aircraft, albeit not particularly competitive compared to Western-built aircraft. In recent times, however, because the nation has lost its role as a global power (its GDP is 10% that of the United States and about the same as Brazil's), the nation is in a different position from where it was twenty years ago.

There is also an inherent tension within the country between (1) those who accept the reality that Western aircraft are very good so it is better to buy those aircraft if the nation wants to develop an efficient airline system and (2) those who see that developing its own civil aircraft industry is an important part of the country's economic progression.

As nations develop, the lobby from the airline industry to be allowed to buy competitive products (Western aircraft) tends to become stronger. There was some evidence of that happening in Russia, and one can speculate that it would become more important in China as well.

Having said that, Russia is now aiming to recreate its civil aircraft manufacturing industry. Its mechanism for doing this is, however, similar to that of China: assembling parts into an aircraft with subcontractors from the West. This is unlikely to create a product that is competitive against Western incumbents.

The current Russian government's desire to fund and support the civil aircraft industry is expensive. As dissent is suppressed, the funding is likely to continue, but sooner or later, the basic economic realities will prevail and the government may have to stop support.

The discussion about Russia draws to a close the review of country support approaches for civil aircraft industries. In the next section, we will compare and contrast the support rationales for the various countries and draw some conclusions about the major themes.

Government Support Rationale and Level of Economic Development

The most often-cited rationales for state intervention in the civil aircraft sector for each of the countries examined above are mapped in Chart 7.1.

Comparison on government support rationales

Rationale / Country ->	US	UK	Germany	Canada	Brazil	Russia	Japan	China
Public good (Defense)	H	M			L	H	L	H
Capital Market failure		M	M	M	H		M	
Technology diffusion	L	L	L	L	M		H	M
Industry targeting	H	L	M	H	H	H	H	H
Strategic Trade Theory		M	H			M		M
Job protection / creation		L	M	M			L	
Level the playing field		L	L	H	M			

Key		
	H	High importance
	M	Medium
	L	Low
		Minimal

Source: Author construction

Chart 7.1. Importance of Various Mechanisms for Government Intervention to Support the Civil Aircraft Industry

The different approaches adopted by developed versus developing nations are significant. Europe and Canada have tended to move the focus of justifications to a more protectionist stance. Both the Canadian and European civil aircraft industries lobby for funding on jobs-protection and level-playing field reasons.

The other difference in funding justifications between developing and developed nations is the role of the stakeholders. In developing nations, the government tends to take the lead initiating the creation of a civil aircraft industry. In developed nations, the industry has to justify (i.e., lobby) for investment monies. The arguments used by the industry firms are likely to center on the issues of capital market failure and protectionism. The notable exception is the United States, where the country's grand strategic imperative predominates.

Most nations with well-developed industries, such as Europe and Japan, accept the capital market-failure rationale. To compensate for failure, they provide development funding in return for loan repayments or royalties on future engine sales. The United States has no such mechanism. Because there is no evidence of lobbying by US producers for such support, my conclusion is that they find acceptable the current policy of military and "basic" research grants.

There is no evidence as yet for the adoption of strategic trade theory arguments beyond Europe to justify funding the civil aircraft sector. One would expect these to eventually emanate from Asia, China in particular, following the Airbus model, but this has not occurred.

Developing nations' governments see the civil aircraft sector as one that provides substantial spin-off in terms of technology and human-factor endowment for their economies. In these cases, governments tend to take the lead in developing domestic capabilities. The aim of policies to encourage technology diffusion is to spread the learning of new skills to many companies within the nation. For Japan, this meant that government intervention was aimed at spreading the new knowledge to companies in the same sector (i.e., competitors). The results produce good technology diffusion but weak individual competitor strength in a global context. A nation with a government policy fostering wide technology diffusion is unlikely to produce a company capable of competing with the incumbents.

In developed nations, the technology-diffusion argument is weaker because the overall technical capabilities of the nation are already high. In this case, the incumbents take the lead and lobby for funding on the grounds of capital market failure and on the arguments of the more emotive jobs protection and level playing field. For the most part, these arguments are successful. It is unusual to see the government of a developed country turn down a funding request from its civil aircraft manufacturer.

The United States does not fit well with the above framework. The US approach to civil aircraft and, more generally, aerospace is one derived from being a superpower. A world-leading indigenous defense capability is required to support the country's doctrine of defense through technological superiority. The thriving civil aircraft industry in the United States is a fortunate beneficiary of that nation having the largest defense sector in the world.

Chapter Summary

This chapter reviewed the various rationales for government intervention and considered the reality of individual country approaches. Developing nations tend to adopt industry-targeting and technology-diffusion approaches, which are driven by government. In developed nations, the companies will often take the lead and seek funding for justifications based on capital market failure, leveling the playing field, and job creation. Finally, we concluded that a developing country that deploys a national-champion support focus is likely to be more successful in creating an international competitor than is a country deploying a technology-diffusion approach.

In Chapter 8, we will address some additional important aspects of entry barriers to the civil aircraft industry that do not fit neatly into the analytical frameworks considered in this chapter.

8.

Additional Aspects of Entry Barriers to the Civil Aircraft Industry

This short chapter closes the subject of entry barriers. It addresses two areas that do not neatly fit into the framework considered earlier but that are nonetheless important when considering industry entry[1]: the partnering strategy paradox and the geostrategic considerations the United States' and China's role in the world.

The Partnering Strategy Paradox

"Partnering strategy paradox" is the term I will use to describe the Catch-22 situation a company will find itself in if it partners with an incumbent. This will be part of their technology-acquisition strategy to become an industry leader itself. The paradox arises because as the company acquires more civil aircraft design skills, it inevitably becomes more commercially linked to its partner (an incumbent). In economic terminology, as time passes, the technological entry barriers to becoming a prime actor in the industry are reduced but the commercial exit cost of breaking a relationship with the partnering incumbent increases (Chart 8.1).

The paradox taken to its logical extreme produces an interesting result: If a firm has the ambition to become an independent new entrant, it should not partner with an incumbent. There are two provisos for this statement: First, when the partnering incumbent sees no threat to its own interests, it will allow the new firm to enter. Second, when an aspirant has sufficient financial backing to be able to withstand the withdrawal of the incumbent's business (which may be the case with China) it can ignore the commercial leverage of the incumbent.

Partnership Strategy Paradox

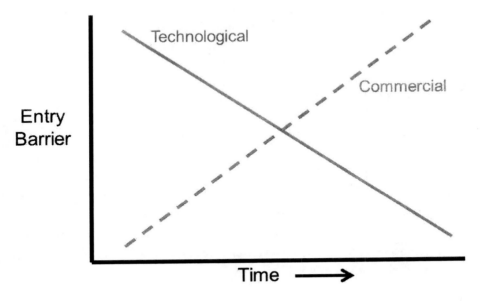

Source: Author construction

Chart 8.1. The Partnering Strategy Paradox

The Exercising of Power over Partners by Incumbents in the Partnering Strategy Paradox

To illustrate the exercise of power in the partnering strategy paradox, we will use an example from the aero engine industry. In the mid-1990s, Snecma (now part of Safran) was probably the most advanced aero engine partner company in the world and was the fourth largest engine company in terms of sales. Snecma aspired to become an independent civil engine company. To achieve this aim, the company adopted a partnership strategy of steadily taking on the more and more technologically challenging parts of the engine. The company Snecma partnered with was aero engine industry leader GE. On the surface, this appears to be a rational strategy for reaching an objective of prime status. As time went by, however, the reliance of Snecma on workload (engineering and manufacturing) from

91

GE's programs meant that the larger company could exert influence over the French company. The instrument of power of the incumbent in this type of relationship, although hardly ever articulated publicly, is the withdrawal of existing workload, which could threaten the aspirant company's finances. For example, more than 65% of Snecma's revenues were reliant on partnering on GE engine programs.

The CFM-XX engine debacle between GE and Snecma provides a case study of how this prime can wield power over a partner.[2] Table 8.1 shows the chronology of the incident. The CFM-XX was going to be a French-led engine program for the Airbus A340-600 aircraft program. Initially, Snecma thought it had realized its ambition of leading a commercial aircraft engine program, only to be thwarted by the actions of its partner, GE. Snecma believed it had the technical capabilities to lead such a development program. The French government, Snecma's owners at the time, was supporting the strategy with development funding support of FFr 2 billion, approximately $400 million.

Table 8.1. Chronology of Engine Selection for the A340-600

10 May 1994
Snecma indicates that it wishes to lead on creating a large civil aero engine. It had raised the issue with GE, and the response "has not been unfavorable." An engine for the proposed Airbus A340-600 was one of the options.

31 Jan 1995
Snecma announces that it is to lead the CFM56-XX program for the A340-600. Bernard Dufour, Snecma's new president, makes it clear that his company will lead the program.

28 Feb 1995
Snecma's vice president of engineering indicates that the "56" designation will be dropped because the engine proposed by Snecma for the A340-600 was a new concept based on a Snecma engine technology demonstrator.

7 Mar 1995
B. Dufour says that he is open to Rolls-Royce and MTU (of Germany) joining the CFM-XX program.

20 Jun 1995
B. Dufour reveals, "We are in the process of looking at contractual conditions of the collaboration (with GE on the CFM-XX)."

26 Sep 1995
The French government agrees to loan Snecma FFr 2 billion ($370m) in reimbursable loans to help develop the CFM-XX engine.

24 Oct 1995
The press reports rumors that Snecma wants to reduce its commitment to GE's GE-90 program, where it is a 25.05% risk and revenue sharing partner. This engine would power the Boeing 777.

29 Jan 1996
Snecma officials announce that they are planning to reduce their share of the GE-90 program.

16 Apr 1996
GE announces an exclusive deal with Airbus to study an engine for the A340-600

30 April 1996
Snecma announces that it will maintain its stake in the GE-90. It also announces that it is linking with Pratt and Whitney to develop a small engine that will compete directly with GE's CF34.

29 May 1996
B. Dufour is fired from his presidency of Snecma. Press coverage focuses on the strategy aimed at breaking the relationship with partner GE. One French press report suggests that Jack Welch, the chairman of GE, let it be known that as long as Dufour was head of Snecma, cooperation with GE would be limited strictly to existing programs. Another report suggests that Welch had made the removal of Dufour one of the conditions of a sixty-aircraft order for Airbus aircraft by GECAS (a subsidiary of GE).

3 Sep 1996
GE states that Snecma will be invited to participate in the engine program for the A340-600. A GE spokesman says relations with Snecma are "much improved" since the departure of Dufour.

13 Jan 1997
Snecma announces that it will participate in a new version of the
GE-90 program and in the proposed GE engine program for the
A340-600 (the GE-XX).

25 Feb 1997
GE announces that discussion with Airbus regarding an engine for the
A340-600 has been abandoned.

25 Mar 1997
Snecma announces that it is in "very positive" negotiations with Rolls-
Royce to participate in the Trent 500 engine proposal for the A340-
600.

22 Jul 1997
Snecma announces that it has declined to participate in the RR Trent
500 engine program. A Snecma spokesman is quoted as saying, "We
have nothing against Rolls-Royce, but you cannot sleep with everybody."

Although the linkages have to be inferred, the public-domain information available is indicative of GE using its leverage to exercise power over Snecma to a remarkable degree. GE bypassed Snecma and negotiated directly with Airbus regarding GE's own engine proposals. At the same time, Snecma was trying to reduce its share of the GE-90 program. Within a few months of outlining Snecma's new direction, the architect of the independent strategy, Snecma President Bernard Dufour, had been sacked. Furthermore, the company was signing up for the next variant of the GE-90 and GE's engine proposal for the A340-600. Based on this anecdotal evidence, it appears that GE effectively had a veto over Snecma strategic development in the commercial sector, at least in larger engines.

The lesson to be learned from this experience is that entry into a market is much more difficult than simply acquiring technological skills. A partnering strategy for a new entrant will enable the new entrant to acquire technological skills from working with an incumbent and, these capabilities could ultimately be developed to such a degree that the new partner believes that it could lead an engine program itself. But this ignores the commercial realities of the new partner's current business, which will be dependent on the relationship with the incumbent. A rational incumbent is unlikely to allow a partner to become a direct competitor and will therefore utilize leverage through its relationship with the partner to stop such an eventuality.

What can we learn from this anecdote? We can conclude that as the technological barriers are reduced for industry entry at prime level, the barriers to exit the existing relationship with an incumbent increase.

The implications of the partnering strategy paradox for the new entrant to civil aircraft manufacturing are counterintuitive. If companies partner with incumbents to acquire technical capabilities, they adopt strategies that could ensure that they will not become independent competitors.

Geostrategic Considerations

This section addresses the little-researched area of geopolitical influences on commercial decisions. Two aspects will be considered: (1) the role of the United States in providing the defense umbrella to East Asia and (2) the strategic intent of China and its potential impact on commercial decisions.

The United States' Role in East Asian Defense

The United States provides a defense umbrella of various forms to Japan, South Korea, and Taiwan. This has two consequences for these nations. First, there is a strong pressure on these countries to purchase military equipment that is compatible with that of the US defense forces'. As a result, much of the military hardware in Japan, South Korea, and, to a lesser extent, Taiwan is either purchased directly from the United States or is a license-built variant of US design. New programs are invariably coproduced with the United States. The effect of these East Asian nations' requirement to develop their own indigenous military civil aircraft design capability is to weaken their efforts in the civil industry. This means that the defense-to-civil technology transfer that takes place in the US civil aircraft industry cannot happen in these East Asian countries.

The second consequence to a US defense umbrella is that although Japan and South Korea are allowed to license-build American equipment, they are not allowed to export these products. In the case of Japan, this is a self-imposed ban, but the result is that neither Japan nor South Korea can establish economies of scale in their defense production because of the lack of additional volume from exports. The overall impact on an East Asian nation of adopting a US defense umbrella is that it has to relinquish some freedom to design and develop products in which the United States has a strategic interest.

China's Strategic Intent

What sets China apart from other East Asian nations is its self-belief that it should rank amongst the great powers the world. This belief has its roots in the long history of the nation, which until 150 years ago led in agricultural productivity, industrial innovation, and standard of living. The fall from eminence from China's perspective could be blamed on the United Kingdom, Japan, Russia, and the United States, who, through various historic episodes, have each weakened the nation. Both the United Kingdom and Russia are diminished actors on the world stage, so today, Japan and the United States dominate geostrategic thinking within Chinese leadership. The interaction between these nations will define China's position as potential superpower or regional power over the next fifty years.

By its actions, the Chinese aim to be, at a minimum, a regional power. For instance, China has acquired air-refueling technology and aims to have a significant fleet of fighter plans and bombers that can be refueled. Additionally, the nation has acquired an aircraft carrier as part of an aspiration to have a blue-water navy of oceangoing vessels.

How does China's geopolitical aspirations of creating a defense aerospace industry to rival that of the United States impact its aspirations for civil market entry? The theme of this book is seeing civil aircraft industry entry in the context of a national industrial policy to upgrade technological capability. An alternative (or additional) framework could be constructed to see civil market entry as an aid to China's military aspirations within aerospace. To be a world power, China needs to have an independent military capability that can project force over long distances. One can therefore hypothesize that China's efforts to enter civil aircraft manufacturing via partnerships with Western companies is an element of its defense-sector entry. This is the concern of export-control agencies in the West and explains why any relationship involving aircraft technology with Chinese companies gets such heavy scrutiny.

Chapter Summary

This chapter draws a conclusion to our consideration of entry barriers from both theoretical and practical perspectives. Entry into the civil aircraft industry is hard. There are three types of entry barrier. First are the well-known barriers of producing competitive civil aircraft, in which companies need to be operating at the technological barrier. Second, and less well known, are the barriers from financial, commercial, and governmental aspects; clearly, government's role is pervasive in civil aircraft manufacturing. Finally is the little-researched area of geopolitical strategy, which is particularly important in the cases of the United States and China.

In Chapter 9, we are going to look at how the civil aircraft industries of various countries/regions were established. We will start with the well-known incumbents of the United States and Europe and consider the more recent entrants from Brazil and Canada. This will lead us to examine the current attempts at industry entry from Japan, China, and Russia.

9.

Civil Jet Aircraft Industry Entry: The Incumbents

In this chapter, we will examine the successful entry strategies of the incumbent civil jet aircraft manufacturers, starting with Boeing of the United States and Airbus from Europe. Then we will address the more recent entrants of Canada and Brazil. Then, in Chapter 10, we will consider the current attempts at industry entry by Japan, China, and Russia.

The aim of this chapter is not explore each country's civil aircraft industry's history in detail. For those interested in more detailed analysis of the civil aircraft companies, I have included several excellent books on the subject in the bibliography, but here, we are going to focus on the key milestones on the way to initial industry entry and then consider any salient developments thereafter.

The United States

The clear leader in civil aviation in the United States is Boeing. Its history goes back to the early part of last century, but in terms of civil jet aircraft participation, its positioning came about from a fortuitous confluence of events after World War II.

World War II saw several major innovations in aircraft design, including all-metal aircraft and the gas turbine jet engine being introduced at the end of the war. These innovations signaled major changes in the configuration of aircraft. For example, innovation in aircraft engines meant there were three potential technological directions for aircraft propulsion. First, an aircraft manufacturer could stick with the piston engine. (An aircraft piston engine is similar in concept to the engine that powers an automobile or SUV.) That technology was mature and had limitations, however. The gas turbine provided the other two aircraft propulsion options. Introduced in the last year of World War II, it was the technology that was going to take the industry forward.[1] The gas turbine engine had a higher power-to-weight ratio than a piston engine and could operate at higher altitudes.

The open question at the time regarding the gas turbine was whether the future was going to be the more fuel-efficient turboprop gas turbine configuration or the turbofan configuration. In the turboprop configuration, the gas turbine itself, which produces the power, is connected to a gearbox at the front of the engine. This gearbox drives a propeller which provides the thrust. Most people are familiar with this setup on smaller aircraft. This arrangement has the advantage of being more fuel-efficient. At the time, this was the option that many people thought would be the leading engine type.

The alternative configuration was to put a direct-drive fan instead of a gearbox on the front of the gas turbine. This produced thrust that would propel the aircraft faster. In fact, it was very fast compared to a turboprop but was not as fuel-efficient. The advantage of the turbofan was that it enabled the aircraft to complete more flights over a given time, so it had a productivity advantage.

At the time, these three power-plant types were being considered by many incumbent aircraft manufacturers who were very familiar with piston engines. They had to make a strategic decision on whether to stick with a piston engine or advance with a turboprop or turbofan. There was some reticence amongst the incumbents to go forward with a new engine type because they had so much vested in pistons engines (i.e., the exit costs were high).

While this was happening, Boeing, which had traditionally not been strong in civil aircraft, saw this propulsion change as an opportunity. Boeing did have a strong position in military turbojet business.[2] It was producing the B-47 Stratojet, which was a transporter for the Department of Defense, and also the B-52 bomber for the Strategic Air Command missions. Both these aircraft were jet-engine powered, so it seemed a straightforward task for Boeing, unencumbered by an existing piston business, to enter the civil sector, and this is what it did.

Boeing developed a dual-use (i.e., military and civilian) prototype called the Model 367-80, which flew on 15 July 1954.[3] This was financed largely at the company's own expense and risk, but with assistance from the government via a research and development (R&D) recovery mechanism of defense contracts.[4] The prototype had few windows and no seats but did have large cargo doors all ready for a military tanker configuration. Just a week after the first flight of the 367-80, the US Air Force ordered 29 military tankers, which became the KC-135. The civil version, called the 707, was ordered on 14 October 1954 by Pan American Airlines. The 707 did require significant structural changes from the 367-80 prototype, but the timings meant that when production began on the tankers, much of the teething problems were resolved at the government's expense. Furthermore, Boeing's President William Allen then convinced the government that having the KC-135 and the 707 on the same production line would save money.[5] The Boeing 707 entered service with Pan American in 1958 and went on to spawn several other aircraft, becoming Boeing's highly successful entry into the civil jet aircraft sector.

The 707 saw two major aircraft derivatives. Using the 707 fuselage, the Boeing 727 was developed. This three-engined aircraft was a medium-ranged aircraft that was successful commercially, with more than 1,800 delivered. In 1968, a twin/two-engined aircraft called the Boeing 737 entered service. The 737 is still in production today, with more than 9,000 produced.

Another major aircraft from Boeing was the 747, which has had a very successful life. Visually, the aircraft is well known for the bump at the front of the fuselage. That bump exists because one of the initial requirements for the aircraft was that the nose on the front of the aircraft would lift to enable cargo to be taken onboard. This went back even to the initial concept of the aircraft, which was to be a large transport aircraft for the US Air Force. Boeing was competing against Douglas, General Dynamics, and Lockheed to provide a large airlifter aircraft. In the end, Boeing did not win that contract, which was ultimately won by Lockheed with the C-5 Galaxy aircraft, powered by GE TF39 engines (which were later derived by GE into the civil CF6 engine). Although Boeing lost the campaign to win the US Air Force airlifter mission requirement, it was left with technology that it could spin off into the civil aircraft market, and that eventually became the Boeing 747.[6]

As time went on, it became clear that the Boeing 727 and 707 would need to be replaced. Boeing's decision was to run near-concurrent development programs to replace these aircraft, which eventually became the Boeing 757 and 767. It was a remarkable feat to run two aircraft programs together nearly at the same time.

The 757 was born of an internal US domestic airline requirement. It was thought at the time that passenger growth within the existing route structure would need to be accommodated with a larger aircraft type, so the concern was that the 737 was at risk of being too small. The government enacted the Deregulation Act in 1978, however, essentially meaning that there was no regulation stopping market entry for new airlines. Thereafter, there were many new airline entrants, which led to the first deployment of the efficient hub-and-spoke route network system used by most US airlines.

The net effect of these changes was that average aircraft size requirements went down domestically in the United States. This was bad news for the Boeing 757 but good news for the 737. Thereafter, the 757 program struggled for many years to gain traction, though it did have a good run in Europe with many of the charter airlines. The 757 was not one of the greatest successes of the Boeing family; nevertheless, eventually, the line eventually produced more than 1,000 of them.

The 767 was an all-new aircraft and owed little of its heritage to the 707. This program was the first one in which partnering was significant on an aircraft. The 767 saw Aeritalia of Italy (now Leonardo) became a partner on the aircraft. It also saw Japan's participation in the aircraft via a joint venture called Civil Transport Development Corporation. The idea of a joint venture of several Japanese companies can be traced back to that government's policy of fostering technology diffusion within their industry. That was an early route for the Japanese to gain aircraft manufacturing expertise.

More recently, Boeing has launched what is now known as the 777. That is an all-new aircraft, but the original concept was to stretch the existing 767. Boeing took the proposal of the stretched/re-engined 767 aircraft to its customer base. That proposal did not meet the customer requirements, so Boeing eventually produced the new 777.

The development of the 777 is worthy of note because Boeing consulted the airlines at a very early stage in the design of the aircraft. The company had an advisory board of eight airlines, and they were involved with the design of the aircraft. This goes to the point that we considered in early chapters about complex product systems (CoPS); as aircraft had become extremely complicated, there was a need for a more intimate relationship with customers to hone the design. This was done to make sure that Boeing produced an aircraft that met diverse market requirements of many airlines.

Finally, let us consider another example of market requirements and how they can change. The next aircraft to be developed by Boeing went on to become the Boeing 787. Before developing the 787, however, Boeing was considering developing a very fast aircraft known as the Sonic Cruiser. It did garner some interest from airlines around the world but the company struggled to achieve the required performance (ie range, operating economics). In addition the economic consequences of the terrorist acts of 9/11 and the increase in fuel prices made that concept uncompetitive, so Boeing went back to a more traditional aircraft design that became the 787. Even though the 787 was of a more traditional than groundbreaking design, it pioneered some radical changes in aircraft design, materials used, and supply chain structure.[7]

We can see that Boeing's approach has been a mixture of opportunism and technological innovation. In the early days, the cross-feeding of technology from its military airlifter expertise to the civil aircraft was a major element of Boeing's successful entry. As the company's product strategy has evolved, a mixture of derivative and new aircraft has been brought to market. One of the success factors of Boeing is this interaction of being both opportunistic and timely with technology embodiment. This enables the company to produce a product that customers want.

Europe

In this section, the major countries we will consider are the United Kingdom, France, Germany, and Holland.[8] We will look at the United Kingdom in detail because it is representative of what happened in other nations.

What we see today in Europe is a consolidated industry under the banner of Airbus,[9] but that concept has taken decades to coalesce from the fragmented national aviation industries. Similar to the US industry, everything started near the end of World War II.

At the beginning of the war, the United States and the United Kingdom had agreed that there would be an allocation of responsibilities in the creation of aircraft for the war effort; the United Kingdom would concentrate on bombers, whereas the United States would concentrate on transportation aircraft. After World War II, this approach reaped advantages for the United States because the country had an industry that could be readily converted to civil aircraft manufacturing. The United Kingdom could not easily convert bombers to civil aircraft, however.

In 1942, the Brabazon Committee[10] was created by the UK government to make recommendations for the future of the civil aviation industry in the United Kingdom after World War II. The government was concerned about this issue because the United Kingdom still had the remnants of an empire and still had aspirations to operate on a global scale. Because it still had an empire to connect, it felt that it had to have a competitive civil aircraft industry.

The committee recommended that several aircraft types be produced by the UK industry. One has to remember that the state pervaded everything in the industry at the time. The state was going to fund these civil aircraft and the state-owned airlines—British Overseas Airway Corporation (BOAC) and British European Airways (BEA)—would purchase the aircraft from a nascent civil jet aircraft industry.

The committee recommended the development of several aircraft. The most successful of these was the Vickers Viscount turboprop aircraft, but, very importantly for the industry, the de Havilland Comet was born out of this study. The de Havilland Comet was the first-ever civil jet-engine-powered aircraft to enter service, in 1952 with BOAC. It flew across the Atlantic. It was very innovative but did suffer from a problem unknown at the time, called metal fatigue. This led to several crashes, and as a result, the fleet was grounded.[11] This enabled competing aircraft, most notably the Boeing 707, to get a foothold in the industry.

It is worth noting that Boeing did actually visit the United Kingdom to examine the Comet. In those early days of the jet industry, there still was a lot of cooperation for the fast-evolving technology.

After the technical success of the Comet (and the Viscount), the British aerospace industry was urged to produce other aircraft. While this was proceeding, the government was gently encouraging the consolidation of the UK industry. It was a large industry scaled to support the war effort. There was a tremendous overcapacity, so there was an economic need for industrial consolidation.

During this tumultuous time in the 1960s, several aircraft were produced from the UK industry, most notably the Vickers VC10 long-range rear four-engined aircraft, the Hawker Siddeley Trident, and the British Aerospace BAC-111. These three aircraft were successful technically but ultimately failed financially because they were tailored by the home airlines of BEA and BOAC. Unfortunately, the aircraft were optimized for the routes of those two airlines, and that limited their applicability to other airlines.

Ultimately, the United Kingdom, through the company British Aerospace Corporation, started some initial designs of a supersonic airliner, which was merged through a joint venture with the French industry, which went on to become the Concorde.

France also had its own aircraft industry immediately after the war. European manufacturing was still operating on a national scale. The problem with this was that the development costs were becoming so high that the economics were just not working. It was difficult to bring a business case together on domestic demand alone.

The French industry had a similar consolidation as the United Kingdom. The industry had been decimated from the Occupation. The remaining industry was small and was directed by the government.

The most important French civil jet aircraft at the time was the Caravelle, which was produced by Sud Aviation and entered service in 1959. It was successful in Europe and even made some headway in the United States. Like the UK industry, the French industry was looking for the next technological lead in civil aircraft and was considering its own supersonic aircraft. As mentioned earlier, this activity was merged with the UK effort to produce the Concorde. Sud Aviation was merged with Nord Aviation in 1970 and became Aérospatiale.

Concorde was an important aircraft because it was the first supersonic civil aircraft. Some would argue that the Russian Tupolev Tu-144 was the first supersonic civil aircraft, but the Tu-144 flew in service for only seven months, whereas Concorde flew for more than 25 years. The aircraft was also important because it produced technology that would be spun off into the Airbus grouping that was going to be created out of the European industry. In addition, the joint venture that produced Concorde was an important precursor of the corporate structure initially developed for Airbus.

Germany's industry was decimated during World War II. It never did produce a civil jet aircraft in its own right, although it came very close through a company called Vereinigte Flugtechnische Werke (VFW). It worked in a joint venture with the Dutch company Fokker to produce a small aircraft called the VFW 614. Only nineteen aircraft were produced, however, so the program was not a success.

The German industry was an important supplier of components and aero structures to the European industry. As elsewhere, the German industry was consolidated into an entity, this one called Messerschmitt-Bölkow-Blohm (MBB), which was then bought by Daimler-Benz as part of an industrial strategy to become a transportation company (which eventually unraveled).

In the year 2000, Daimler-Benz Aerospace became part of the European Aeronautic Defence and Space Company (EADS), which was a consolidation of the French and German civil aircraft industries and the UK part of Airbus. As mentioned in previous chapters, this effort was characterized by the Europeans' imperative to create an industry that would compete on a world scale against the United States.

The other company worth mentioning here is from Holland. The Dutch company Fokker had an illustrious history going back to World War I and was the largest producer of aircraft in the world during the 1930s. It was badly damaged during the German occupation during World War II but did reconstitute itself and became a viable small civil aircraft manufacturer. It produced the turboprop aircraft called the F27 and the turbofan-powered aircraft called the F28.

Both the F27 and the F28 had support from the home government. At a later stage, both of these aircraft needed upgrading, and Fokker took the unwise step of upgrading both at the same time. The aircraft were re-engined with newer, higher-technology engines. The F28 was stretched to become the F100, and the F27 became the F50. The effort put Fokker under financial strain. Ultimately, the company ran out of money and was consolidated into the German industry through Deutsche Aerospace AG (DASA), but DASA was having its own financial problems through parent Daimler-Benz, and it was decided that Fokker would have to stop making aircraft. This was a big blow to the Dutch pride and ended civil aircraft manufacturing in Holland.

As we come to the end of this section on Europe, we need to briefly consider some geopolitical issues and their implications. At the end of World War II, Europe's economies were decimated. Beyond that was the mounting threat of the spread of communism from the Union of Soviet Socialist Republics (USSR). The United States acted first in 1948 by stabilizing Europe with economic aid via the Marshall Plan, which provided over $100 billion (in today's dollars) of stimulus to its ailing nations. Second, and more importantly for the theme of this book, the United States facilitated the creation of the North Atlantic Treaty Organization (NATO). This organization is a military alliance of mutual defense and includes the United States and European countries. Signatories of the treaty agreed that an attack on one country was an attack on them all (Article 5). This has effectively locked the United States into defense of Europe. From the US perspective, this makes sense because the European economies are key markets for the nation. It is less costly for the United States to be imbedded with Europe to create a credible deterrence than to have to come to Europe's aid at a later date.

The resultant behavior from these geopolitical effects is that European governments have had less of a need to develop a large defense capability because they can call upon that of the United States. The impact on Europe's aerospace industry is that it has fewer opportunities to derive technology from defense products. This goes some way toward explaining why Europe's government funding mechanisms appear highly supportive to civil aircraft when compared to the funding mechanisms of the United States.

What we learn from the European experience is that their governments—whether British, French, German, or Dutch—were heavily involved in supporting and encouraging the development of the civil aircraft industry. Government was heavily engaged in producing the Comet, the first civil jet aircraft to enter passenger service. It was also heavily involved in the establishment and facilitation of Airbus.

Canada

Canada was a surprisingly late entrant into the civil airliner business. It has a long, illustrious history in aviation going back to the 1920s with Vickers and de Havilland, both companies from the United Kingdom, with subsidiaries in Canada established to build aircraft for the Canadian defense requirement.

The first Canadian company to produce a civil airliner was Canadair.[12] The company provides an interesting history lesson in industrial policy. In 1944, Canadian Vickers Limited, the British-owned subsidiary, was sold to the Canadian government, and Canadair was born. That company was making license-built American aircraft and flying boats for the specific requirements of the Canadian hinterland.

Very quickly thereafter, in 1946, the Electric Boat Company in the United States bought Canadair and in 1954 bought Convair, a US aircraft company. This entity, along with several other purchases and acquisitions, became General Dynamics.

As an aside, Convair had a slight dalliance with the civil aircraft industry in the United States, producing two aircraft called the Convair 880 and then the 990 during the 1960s. Neither program was successful, and Convair later exited the civil aircraft industry to concentrate on aero structures.

General Dynamics had a change of strategic direction, which resulted in the Canadian government reacquiring Canadair in 1976. At this stage, the Canadair was considering developing a business jet, which became the Challenger 600 (which is still in production today). The Challenger 600 was initially designed by Bill Lear and was known as the LearStar 600 in its very formative design phase; Canadair bought the concept from him around 1978.

These intellectual property rights and the brand of Lear were used by Canadair to convince the Canadian government that it had an excellent design for a business jet. Canadair was successful and convinced the government under Prime Minister Jean Chretien to provide some funding for the development of the aircraft. This took the form of direct government support for R&D and the aircraft, which was eventually certified in 1980.

In the Canadian aerospace scene and context, it is important to talk about what is known as the Avro Arrow debacle and what is known as Black Friday in Canadian aerospace industry parlance. At the end of World War II, Canada's aerospace industry still had aspirations to be independent, in having its own defense capability. A company called Avro,[13] which was British-owned at the time, was developing a supersonic air fighter, which was to be called the Avro Arrow.

This was at a time when there was a great uncertainty about how the West was going to be defended via a nuclear deterrent. Was the nuclear device going to be delivered by an aircraft or a missile? In 1957, this was resolved for Canada with an agreement with the United States for Canada to join North American Aerospace Defense Command (NORAD), the early-warning defense system of the United States. Part of this agreement was to potentially put some missiles into Canada as the country's share of the defense burden.

It became apparent, however, that Canada could not afford to both participate in its own indigenous fighter aircraft design and also fund its obligations to NORAD, so in 1959, the Avro Arrow aircraft program was canceled. The day of that cancellation in 1959 is known in the Canadian aerospace world as Black Friday. The indigenously designed Orenda Iroquois jet engine for the Arrow was also canceled at the same time. The weekend after the announcement saw 15,000 staff laid off from Avro, and probably on the order of another 15,000 were laid off in the supply chain. This created a political furor at the time. The decision was not changed, but the topic continues to be sensitive to this day within the aerospace community. Many of those individuals who were laid off diffused into other companies or left Canada. Some engineers went across the border to the United States and participated in their space program. Others went to Europe and participated in programs such as Concorde.

From the "Canada, Inc." perspective, an important consequence of Black Friday was a loss of highly talented individuals from the country. This episode hangs in the background over every major government decision about the aerospace scene in Canada. The removing of the need for an independent military aircraft industry naturally led the focus to be switched to the civil sector. With this context, it is understandable that civil aircraft programs now receive sympathetic attention from the government. This set the scene for Canadair to be supported by the government.

After the Challenger 600 business jet was developed and certified in 1980, Canadair was privatized (1986) and became part of Bombardier. Bombardier started looking at a regional jet version of the Challenger 600. This transitioned into an aircraft that would become known as the CRJ 100 and would provide Canada's entry in the civil jet industry.

The creation of the CRJ 100 involved a stretch of the Challenger 600 fuselage.[14] This made the aircraft into a 50-seat civil aircraft. This was in the early days of deregulation, which resulted in the restructuring of the route networks into the hub-and-spoke network. This development stimulated the need for 50-seat jets, so the aircraft did well in the United States. The timing was perfect, and the aircraft entered service in 1992. Bombardier went on to ride the surge of US demand for the CRJ 100 and the later CRJ 200 program.

As with the Challenger 600, the CRJ 100/200 received government support. Later, there was yet another version, a derivative of the CRJ that went back to the business jet sector. This aircraft was called the Bombardier Global Express. Again, there was some government support for this program.

It is interesting to note here that the Global Express deployed an international supply chain, much more so than did prior aircraft. It included Shorts, another subsidiary of Bombardier, based in Northern Ireland and, more importantly in the context of this book, Mitsubishi of Japan to manufacture the wing and the center fuselage. This gave the Japanese company experience in manufacturing major components of civil aircraft.

As we have already learned, creating an aircraft is not as simple as just bolting parts together. Nevertheless, however, Mitsubishi being able to participate in this program was helpful for the Japanese in terms of developing their own capability. We will discuss the Japanese capability further in Chapter 10.

In 1996, Bombardier considered buying Fokker, which was in financial difficulties. Bombardier wanted to transition into aircraft larger than the CRJ 100 and 200, which had already been stretched to become the CRJ 700 and 900 (70-seaters and 90-seaters, respectively). An acquisition of Fokker would have given Bombardier a 100-seater aircraft and potentially a 120-seater aircraft, but this did not happen and Fokker eventually ended up being owned by Daimler-Benz Aerospace.

In 1998, Bombardier considered an all-new aircraft called the BRJ-X, which had about 120 seats. The company canceled that program two years later. A few years later, it revisited this market space and launched a program called the CSeries. This aircraft went into service in 2016 after costly development delays. The CSeries is a slightly bigger aircraft than the BRJ-X, and because of this, Airbus and Boeing consider it a competitor.

It is an interesting aspect of the industry to observe how incumbents react to a new entrant. At the writing of this book, Bombardier is in intense competition with Airbus and Boeing. Bombardier has attempted entry, and we have yet to see whether the CSeries will be successful.

The Canadian entry into the marketplace was similar to the European entry in that its relationship with the United States had created a situation in which there was no need for an indigenous large scale defense-oriented industry; however, there was a recognition that Canada had a lot of aerospace expertise and this expertise created high-wage jobs, which was good for the economy as a whole.

The Canadian government sees the aerospace industry as strategic. This is an unusual statement from a developed nation, but Canada is clear, and its politicians have said many times over the years that the aerospace industry is strategic. One can speculate that there will continue to be some institutional memory about Avro Arrow episode and of jobs migrating across the border to the United States.

Government support for civil aircraft programs is close to assured in Canada. One can observe that the delays in the CSeries program have produced concerns about whether Bombardier can complete that program. Here, the Quebec province has been very forthright in saying that it is willing to support Bombardier,[15] even considering taking an equity stake in the CSeries aircraft program.

Brazil

Brazil's entry into the civil jet aircraft sector was in 1996 with the initial deliveries of the Embraer ERJ 145 to the US-based regional airline Continental Express.[16] This was the culmination of a 46-year journey, which goes to the theme of this book, that entry into civil aircraft manufacturing is hard.

The journey started with the initiation of various technology centers in the early 1950s. A notable visionary at the time, Casimiro Montenegro Filho, a lieutenant colonel in the Brazilian Air Force, was instrumental in setting up what is known as Instituto Tecnológico de Aeronáutica (ITA), the aviation or aeronautical university, in São José dos Campos in 1950. This university is modeled on the Massachusetts Institute of Technology (MIT) experience in the United States. Professor Fred Smith from MIT helped to establish ITA for aeronautical studies. In fact, many of the students from the university went on to run Embraer, which is now so successful on the global stage.

As part of the network of institutions that were established in the 1950s, the Brazilian General Command for Aerospace Technology was also established. This is an overarching organization, and one of its major roles is administering aircraft certification requirements for Brazil; it has a role similar to that of the Federal Aviation Administration in the United States.

111

The other dimension to Brazil's participation in the civil aircraft industry is the large government engagement over the development of the indigenous aircraft industry, but this engagement can be seen as inconsistent at best. Brazil has had civil government presidents and military presidents who were either for or antagonistic to the development of an aircraft industry, variously supporting or holding back the development of this indigenous industry.

Of these various presidents, we should start with Getúlio Vargas, who was president twice, from 1930 to 1945, and 1951 to 1954. He was an aviation enthusiast and flew in many of the early prototypes of Brazilian aircraft that were built and designed within the nation for national requirements.

Empresa Brasileira de Aeronáutica (Embraer) was established in August of 1969, and its main mission at the time was to materialize and bring to market an aircraft called the Bandeirante. This aircraft was based on a project design from one of the ITA institutions established in the 1950s. The design was known as the IPD-6504. The Bandeirante was wholly an indigenous design and with half the value of the parts being brought in from outside of Brazil. The aircraft was designed by Max Holste, a French engineer, in accordance with specifications laid down by the Brazilian Ministry of Aeronautics. The IPD-6504 was an unpressurized, rugged turboprop aircraft capable of carrying around 15–20 passengers. Its timing was fortuitous, as it found sales from the fast-growing US regional airline market.

The Bandeirante was then used as the basis for the next aircraft that Embraer was going to build, the Brazilia. Launched in 1985, the 30-seat Brazilia was built in response to market analysis suggesting that there was demand for bigger turboprops within the regional airline sector. This aircraft did well and at the time was probably one of the most successful Brazilian exports into the United States.

The next aircraft program that was launched was first known as the EMB 145 and later became the ERJ 145. Again, recognizing what was happening in the regional airline world, the company saw a potential requirement for a 50-seat jet aircraft. This is what eventually became Brazil's first civil jet aircraft, a 50-seater aimed at the regional market in the United States.

Domestically in Brazil, there was a lot of political and economic turmoil, so at this time, there was not much support for an indigenous aircraft manufacturer. The first democratically elected president after military government, President Fernando Collor de Mello, had a short presidency, from 1990 to 1992, but was instrumental in the privatization of Embraer, which was imperative so funding could be freed up to ensure its long-term survival as a company.

After several failed attempts, the government sold a 45% stake in the company. The company had a cash injection, the government wrote off $700 million worth of debt, and the company was recapitalized. Within a year or so of Embraer being privatized, the ERJ 145 program was restarted after being postponed due to lack of funding. The aircraft entered service in 1996 and represents the culmination of a 46-year journey for the Brazilian aircraft industry.

The ERJ 145 was supported by 22% development funding with a refundable loan from Banco Nacional de Desenvolvimento Econômico e Social (BNDES) and Finep, both government institutions. One organization provided R&D funding in terms for the loan, and the other provided more traditional lines R&D tax credits and innovation support.

BNDES, a state bank, more controversially also provided sales financing for the ERJ 145. This support became a conflict at a governmental level with Canada. Both countries went to the World Trade Organization with counterclaims of illegal sales support to both countries modifying their civil aircraft support.

After the ERJ 145, Embraer consolidated its position and developed the all-new E-Jet, which was a 70–100-seater regional jet. This yet again was following the trend of regional airline markets that were requiring yet bigger aircraft. The E-Jet eventually replaced the ERJ 145.

One of the major features and successes of Embraer is that it develops aircraft that the market requires. The company is not focused on producing aircraft for domestic needs and does not produce technology for technology's sake. The company is a market-oriented organization, and when on occasion where it has diverted from that strategy, it has learned from that bad experience.

A classic case of this bad experience was with the CBA-123 Vector aircraft in the 1990s, which was a politically inspired aircraft with the partnership of Embraer and the Argentinian company Fábrica Militar de Aviones.

This CBA-123 was a smaller derivative of the Brazilia, a 19-seater with an unusual propulsion solution. Instead of traditional positioning around the wings, in a puller-type configuration , the turboprops were placed at the back of the fuselage in a pusher configuration. Normally, turboprop engines are installed around the wings and are configured in such a way that they are puller-type configurations.

The CBA-123 was a highly innovative aircraft, sophisticated and challenging technically. Because of this, it was expensive and ultimately uncompetitive for the market it was aiming at. It was driven by the Brazilian political situation at the time, which was trying to align with local countries rather than with the United States. As such, the company produced a largely politically driven aircraft that was not successful in a commercial sense but was technologically quite an accomplishment. A lot of technological knowledge that came out of this aircraft went on to be incorporated into the ERJ 145.

It is perhaps worth taking a little detour here to discuss politically inspired civil aircraft. In Chapter 10, we will consider Japan's first attempt to enter the civil aircraft industry, with the YS-11. The YS-11 was a turboprop and is seen as a technological success but a commercial failure. It was expensive and did not find many customers outside of Japan. It was really a program driven more by industrial policy than by market requirements.

A similar experience can be seen with Concorde, the supersonic aircraft jointly built by the United Kingdom and France. Although it was seen that there might be a demand, the market shifted away from the Concorde over its elongated development program. Furthermore, the allocation of work between the partners and the management of the program was political. This led to a non-market orientation, which was one of the reasons for the Concorde's commercial failure, with only 14 aircraft ultimately entering service.

In a way similar to the YS-11 creating the technological bedrock that enabled Japan to partner with Boeing, Concorde generated technology expertise that enabled the United Kingdom and France to contribute to the Airbus project. Similarly, the failure of the CBA-123 in a commercial sense provided technology that enabled the Embraer ERJ 145 to be a success.

One of the lessons one has to learn about civil aircraft is that commercial failure is not all bad, because technology has been developed that can be utilized in other programs. This is a lesson that has been learned many times in aviation, and, I am sure, in other industry sectors, too.

Chapter Summary

This chapter has reviewed the successful entry of the United States, Europe, Canada, and Brazil into the civil jet airliner industry. We can observe two consistent themes from their experiences: First, the role of government engagement is universal. Second, to be successful, an aircraft needs to satisfy a market need rather than a politically driven specification. In Chapter 10, we will consider three countries—Japan, China, and Russia—and their attempts over the years to enter the civil jet aircraft industry.

10.

Civil Jet Aircraft Industry Entry: The Aspirants

In this chapter, we are going to consider three countries—Japan, China, and Russia—and their attempts over the years to enter the civil aircraft industry. All three countries are on the cusp of bringing a civil aircraft to market and being long-term successful. The latter is the ultimate measure of successful industry entry.

Each nation has had a long history in aviation, and each has lessons to be shared about what has failed and what has been successful. These nations are interesting because we can compare their approaches with those nations that have already been successful—the United States, European nations, Canada, and Brazil.

Japan

Let us start with Japan. This country provides a fascinating example because it has a history of being highly successful in entering other manufacturing industries. One of the intriguing questions for this nation that is so technologically savvy is why it does not have its own indigenous civil aircraft program. We will consider the causes for this omission and, in particular, consider some of the policy issues that the government has deployed over the years.

To understand the civil aircraft industry in Japan, we have to go back to World War II. Japan had the fourth largest aircraft industry in the world, behind the United States, the United Kingdom, and Germany. It produced a prodigious amount of aircraft. Mitsubishi's Nagoya plant was the largest in the world at the time.

In August 1945, the Japanese flew a gas turbine-powered aircraft too late to change the course of the war, but it showed how advanced in technology the Japanese were, though, admittedly, the engine and the aircraft were based on German technology. (For instance, the Ishikawajima Ne-20 jet engine[1] was derived from the German BMW 003 aircraft engine.) Nevertheless, the Japanese industry was highly sophisticated at the end of World War II.

Because of this sophistication, Japan was banned from participating in aerospace for seven years after World War II. General MacArthur, the Supreme Commander, abolished all activity in aviation in Japan. A similar ban took place in Germany; both the losers of World War II had their aerospace industries curtailed by the Allies.

One of the effects of this in Japan was that engineers moved into other industries because they could not practice in aerospace. These other industries included bicycle and industrial machinery manufacturing. One could argue that much of the success of other Japanese industries was because of the employment of highly qualified aerospace engineers who were available to use their expertise in less advanced sectors.

Japan is recognized as an example of a government that uses industrial policy. Its industrial policy was deployed from the 1960s through the early 1980s by a government department, the Ministry of International Trade and Industry (MITI). Companies were subsidized via government grants and directed entry into industries that MITI had targeted for growth. Initially, the government's focus was on the steel and ship-building industries. Then it transitioned into the automotive and electronics businesses. Much of this transition was directed by the government.

One of the things that is pertinent in the case of Japan is the country's national ethos. The government, companies, and general population were unified in a common purpose to improve the nation. The impact in terms of government policy is that they were inclined to deploy an industrial policy that has technology diffusion at its heart. This becomes very important when we think about the aircraft industry after World War II.

One of the most important episodes in the Japanese aircraft industry after World War II was the development of the NAMC YS-11.[2] This was a technically successful civil aircraft, but it was turboprop-powered. I do not consider the YS-11 a successful industry entry because it was not sustained. The aircraft ended production, and that was Japan's one and only attempt at indigenous manufacturing of civil aircraft until recently.

Although in this book, we are considering primarily turbofan-powered aircraft, we are taking a closer look into the entry of the YS-11 because there is a lot to be learnt from the YS-11 experience. MITI prompted the YS-11 to be built. The aircraft was the vision of MITI Director Akazawa Shoichi, who argued that Japan should move into civil aircraft manufacturing:

> The base of the mountain [of the aircraft industry] is broad; it is a high-precision industry, so the diffusion of technology will be very great. I considered it a diamond [among industries]. ... A nation without an aircraft industry will never pass as an industrial nation of the first rank.[3]

In 1957, a design research association was formed to lead to the YS-11. Many of the Japanese companies were involved, as were some senior politicians. The industry was very enthusiastic about manufacturing an aircraft, as one can imagine, but sensibly, they insisted on government guarantees of financial support.

The budget for the aircraft was agreed upon and was taken to the Diet in May 1958. The legislation enabled the program to go ahead. The program was led by the complicated joint-venture company called Nihon Aircraft Manufacturing Company (NAMC).

NAMC was structured such that half the shareholding was from the Japanese government and 20% was from manufacturing industries. Of this 20%, about half was from Mitsubishi Heavy Industries, 26% was from Kawasaki Heavy Industries, and 13% was from Fuji Heavy Industries. These were the organizations that were eventually going to produce the aircraft.

The remaining shareholders were an interesting collection of utilities, trading companies, insurance companies, and banks. The company structure strongly suggested that the YS-11 was geared toward technology diffusion, aimed at transitioning aircraft high technology into the general industry in a broad sense. Contrast that with Embraer, which was a government-owned entity for most of its early existence. It became privatized and its initial stockholders were Brazilian pension funds. It is a very different structure from the YS-11 experience.

The first flight of the YS-11 occurred in 1962, but at this stage, development costs were already climbing and the project was over budget. The Ministry of Finance was concerned, and eventually, in late 1961, it cancelled the subsidy program, against MITI's objections.

This action by the Ministry of Finance is worth exploring a little further. Most perceptions about government are that government has one homogenous view of how to deploy policy, but this is not the case in many countries. There are various wings of governing power, and they often have divergent views. That was the case in Japan with the YS-11. There was MITI, which had the role of advocating a policy to support the YS-11, but this needed funding, and that was controlled by the Ministry of Finance, which eventually lost patience with the program and canceled funding the project.

The program struggled on after the Ministry of Finance canceled funding but was about five years late. By the time the YS-11 reached the market, the market requirements had moved on—The YS-11 was a turboprop aircraft, and by this time, turbofans had become the engine of choice. The program was overtaken by events. The YS-11 sold reasonably well to the home market of Japan, but the Japanese market is quite small when compared to that of countries such as the United States.

This is something we will come back to consider as one of the discriminators of a program's success. Is the aircraft solely designed for the home market? The problem with designing for a domestic market is that many times, the market is not big enough to justify financial investment in a new aircraft program. There was not enough domestic market for the YS-11, and this was part of the reason for the Ministry of Finance pulling the plug on the program.

Only 182 YS-11 aircraft were built. The program was widely seen as a technological success, but it was a market and financial failure. In the aftermath of this program, the government changed its strategy toward the nascent aircraft industry. It deployed a strategy of partnership with incumbents, most importantly with Boeing of the United States. As time went by, the Japanese companies took larger shares of Boeing civil aircraft programs, from the 1970s through the present.[4]

These partnerships were encouraged by the Japanese government. The structure for partnership on the Japanese side was often through several companies participating as partners of Boeing. The notion of creating a national champion was not Japan's driving force. The Japanese perspective here was that it was going to develop technology to be spread among many parties.

Over the years, a tension continued between the realities of being subservient in a partnering relationship but still hankering to lead a an aircraft program. From the 1980s through today, the Japanese industry has tried to take more participation in programs, particularly with Boeing. It has also made various attempts of going it alone with indigenous programs, but they never amounted to anything (until very recently).

One example was the Boeing 7J7, which was going to be an aircraft to replace the Boeing 737. The 7J7 was being considered at the time in the 1980s when fuel prices were high, it was concluded that a new high-technology aircraft was required. Fuel prices collapsed, however, and we saw low oil prices in the order of $30 per barrel for about 15 years afterward. Because of this, the 7J7 did not proceed. This event was important to the Japanese because the Japanese were going to take a large share of it. There was also a Japanese program called the YSX, in which Boeing was going to be a junior partner. Yet again, however, that program did not proceed.

At this point, it is worthwhile to reemphasize the idea of entry barriers and the partnership strategy paradox discussed in Chapter 8.[5] Recall that in this paradox, technological entry barriers reduce over time for the junior partner as it gains experience but if it is partnering with a major incumbent, commercial exit barriers exist, often in the form of contractual constraints protecting the incumbent from competition. One of the reasons to have these protections for the incumbent is to enable partnerships to actually happen. If an incumbent does not have those protections, it is not going to partner with a new entrant and thus the new entrant to compete against it.

In more recent years, we have seen another attempt by the Japanese industry to become a civil aircraft manufacturer, with an aircraft called the Mitsubishi Regional Jet (MRJ). Initially, it was going to be an all-composite aircraft, but Mitsubishi decided to change that, which added some time to the development program.

The aircraft will use new engines from Pratt & Whitney that use a geared turbofan concept. When the MRJ program was launched, it was potentially a threat to incumbents Embraer and Bombardier because it is going to be a 70–90-seat jet aircraft.

If we look deeper into the structure of the company bringing the MRJ to market, we find that Mitsubishi has a large shareholding but we also find shareholding by Toyota, Sumitomo Mitsui, and other companies, as well as the Development Bank of Japan. The driving concept of technology diffusion remains but is not as predominant as in the YS-11 experience.

The MRJ has taken many orders, including a large order from the US regional airline SkyWest for 100 aircraft, but much of the order book is from the Japanese airlines All Nippon Airways and Japan Airlines. After the MRJ enters service, the next major milestone of Japan's successful industry entry will be whether Mitsubishi brings another aircraft to the marketplace. It is a tremendous achievement to bring one aircraft to the marketplace, but is Japan's position secure enough and has it made enough money to justify bringing a second aircraft to market? This is a big hurdle, and one is left to wonder whether the Japanese government will lose patience as it did with the YS-11.

It will be interesting to see how this second attempt at entry by Japan will prevail. There is currently a heavy reliance of the Japanese airlines for MRJ production volume. Then, also, there is still some reliance on technology diffusion in the industrial-policy rather than national-champion approach. Finally, there is a concern that the program is late and that system integration issues are causing delays.

It is worthwhile expanding on that latter point. System integration, as mentioned earlier in the book in terms of complex product systems (CoPS), is an entry barrier in its own right. Building or manufacturing wings or fuselages as a subcontractor is a challenge, but assembling them together and having all the internal systems communicate with one another to create a coherent aircraft system is a very demanding capability. Another challenge is that

Mitsubishi has to bring this aircraft to market, and before that, it has to be certified by the FAA to be recognized as a globally acceptable aircraft. These are tough entry barriers. Many people think that entry is fairly straightforward, but achieving certification is a challenge in its own right. Even after certification, the manufacturer has to produce the aircraft economically and move down the learning curve as fast as it can so it can create an economic return on the aircraft.

At the time of the writing of this book, it is too early to judge whether the MRJ will be successful.

Russia

Russia is an embodiment of the classic quote from Lincoln: "Defeat from the jaws of victory." As we will see later in this section, Russia's industry managed to produce a competitive civil aircraft, but the deployment of that aircraft and its ongoing success are in question because of geopolitical developments initiated by Russia. We will consider these later in this section.

Russia's entry into the global civil aircraft industry really got started after the dissolution of the Union of Soviet Socialist Republics (USSR) in December 1991, following the big milestone of the Berlin Wall coming down in November 1989. Prior to December 1991, the Russian aerospace industry was essentially part of a military-industrial complex to support the Soviet Union and had a strongly skewed defense orientation. That orientation incentivized the industry to produce high-performance military machines with high production volumes.

This orientation had little focus on fuel efficiency, and little consideration for the development of profit-generating aircraft. Low maintenance costs and keeping the aircraft operational to maximizing revenue flying hours was therefore a low priority.

The main customer for the civil aircraft industry in the Soviet Union was Aeroflot, the national airline. This model came to an abrupt end once the USSR disintegrated. Russia emerged after the disintegration, but it had a distressed economy, in which the aerospace industry, particularly the civil sector, collapsed. The industry was reduced to producing only a handful of aircraft for many years.

During the Soviet era, the industry was fragmented. Design houses that created aircraft concepts were separate from the manufacturing organizations and factories. In fact, these could be geographically far from one another. The system that made this industrial structure work was the centralized planning departments of the Soviet bureaucracy. After the dissolution of the USSR, this structure collapsed. The design houses and manufacturing facilities were left without leadership and had to create their own survival techniques, which meant on many occasions participating in industries outside of aerospace.

Russia's initial attempts at selling or developing aircraft for the civil market were driven by modifications of old Soviet aircraft. Some replaced the Russian power plants with Western engines and tried to improve the avionics within the aircraft. Both of these technologies were lagging within Russia.

Examples from the mid-1990s include the Ilyushin IL-96 proposal to be powered by a Pratt & Whitney engine, the PW2337, and the Tupolev Tu-204, which was proposed to be powered by the Rolls-Royce RB211-535 with Western avionics. Neither of these programs led to success. Eventually, the Russian industry saw that the way forward was to restructure itself to have a national champion (as we saw with Brazil). This approach led to the development of an indigenous civil aircraft within the confines of a consolidated entity called the United Aircraft Corporation (UAC).

The UAC was a consolidation of the design houses and the manufacturing facilities. Sukhoi, a company with a long, illustrious history in aviation, was designated the civil aircraft manufacturer. In June 2000, there was an initial proposal to partner up with a Western company called Alliance Aircraft, an offshoot from the ailing Fairchild Dornier business. The thinking behind this aircraft concept (which was a 55-seat, 75-seat, 95-seat aircraft family) was for the Russian industry to partner with Western companies to manufacture products that would be acceptable to the certification requirements of the West and to sell in large volumes to make the economics work.

The Alliance route did not work, and within a year or so, Sukhoi was in discussions with Boeing and with Alenia of Italy to bring a similar aircraft family to the marketplace. This grouping was announced at the Paris Airshow in 2001. Boeing was going to act in a consultancy role on marketing, design, certification, and manufacturing. Alenia went on to be involved in some of the manufacturing aspects. Ilyushin of Russia was going to assist in developing the certification requirements.

By October 2003, all major suppliers had been selected. In late 2005, the program had launch orders from a Russian leasing company and Aeroflot, as well as the promise of funding from the Russian government as part of a government program called the Development of Civil Aviation in Russia 2005–2009. The aircraft would later be named Superjet.

The Superjet was developed with help from many Western suppliers. Indeed, some reports suggest that Western supplies account for 70%–80% of the value of the aircraft. These include the engines, much of the avionics, and the landing gear. Much of the aerostructure—the fuselage and wing—were indigenous to Russia, however.

The first flight of the Superjet took place in May 2008, but the final certification of the aircraft was delayed because of problems with the development of the engine called the SaM146. The engine was also part of the Russian industrial policy: The Russian engine company NPO Saturn partnered with the French engine company Snecma in a joint venture called PowerJet (incidentally, its namesake, Power Jets Ltd., was a UK company established in 1944 by Frank Whittle for the purpose of developing the first jet engine).

Finally, in 2011, the aircraft received Russian certification, and in February 2012, it received the important European Aviation Safety Agency (EASA) certification. This European certification enabled the aircraft to be sold and delivered worldwide because EASA certification is the equivalent of FAA certification. An aircraft that has EASA certification can be sold wherever there are FAA requirements.

Unfortunately, during May of 2012, there was a crash of a demonstrator aircraft in Indonesia. This was eventually blamed on pilot error, so the aircraft itself was not the issue. In July 2013, the landing gear of one aircraft collapsed when the aircraft landed and there was some damage to the aircraft.

After these teething problems, the aircraft seemed to enter service reasonably well, considering it was brand-new. (There are always teething problems with the service entry of new aircraft.) There were reports of high maintenance costs and unreliability of the aircraft, but overall, it seemed to be operating well within Russia and with the Mexican airline Interjet.

Several issues have arisen in recent years, however. First, the delay in aircraft certification meant that competing manufacturers launched their own aircraft, most notably the Mitsubishi MRJ and the Embraer E-Jet 2 (second-generation E-Jet). Both these aircraft have the very-latest-technology engines, which makes their fuel usage economically advantageous, so although the Russian aircraft came to market with a reasonably current-technology aircraft, because of delays in getting it into service, Mitsubishi and Embraer could leapfrog the Superjet in terms of technology level.

The more important development was in the geopolitical sphere. Russia, through its surrogates, has invaded a part of the Ukraine and subsumed Crimea. This has had major ramifications for Russia. In particular, economic sanctions have been imposed by the United States and the European Union (EU) that have reportedly had a significant negative impact on the Russian economy.[6]

The US and EU sanctions have not been directed at the Superjet; the Western suppliers to the program can continue to supply parts, and new aircraft are being delivered. What has been a constraint on the Superjet has been the impact on aircraft sales financing. For example, one of the blacklisted organizations is the Eximbank, Russia's state export-import bank. This could reduce the ability of Sukhoi to arrange competitive customer financing to fund the purchase of the Superjet.

In an example of a subtle impact of the sanctions, Superjet customer Air Baltic has delayed its purchase of six aircraft. Air Baltic needed financial support, and it was reported that the Latvian government provided funding on the condition that Air Baltic would not make purchases from countries under international sanctions. It appears Russia will have difficulties selling the Superjet to Western airlines while sanctions are in place.

At the moment, we cannot judge the success of the Superjet. The prospects do not look good, though. That is unfortunate, because the technological heritage of the Russian aircraft industry is excellent. It was positioning itself to sell civil aircraft to the West, but unfortunately, the geopolitical situation intervened and disrupted a good strategy.

This example of Russia helps make a more general point about the globalization of high technology: If you want to sell to the West, you have to abide by the norms acceptable to Western governments. In this sense, globalization of high technology is allowed to happen by governments. From Russia's point of view, they saw the benefits of accessing Western technology. But the political environment changed and Russia now has a product that is difficult to sell in the Western marketplace.

Meanwhile, in a follow-on, an all-new 150-seat aircraft called the Irkut MC-21 is being developed in Russia. Similar to the Superjet, it will have Western components, including Pratt & Whitney PW1400G engines. Russia's aspiration to enter the civil jet industry clearly remains, as made clear by Dmitry Medvedev, Prime Minister of Russia, in 2016:

> The MC-21 is new evidence of Russia's ability to create plans that move our aircraft manufacturing industry forward and allow us to compete with other countries. ... There are very few nations that have aircraft-making industries. They are the top league and we mustn't drop out of it.[7]

China

When considering the Chinese aviation industry,[8] the keys to understanding are the connection to internal governance, geographic scale, and geopolitics. It is within this very broad context that the nation has aspired to develop an indigenous aircraft industry.

The start for the Chinese civil jet industry was in the early 1970s with the thawing of relationships between China and the West, heralded by the visit of President Nixon in 1972. This facilitated the selling of ten Boeing 707 aircraft to China that were delivered to the national airline, Civil Aviation Administration of China (CAAC).[9] The UK company Hawker Siddeley delivered 35 Trident aircraft at the same time.

During this time, the home industry developed an aircraft called the Y-10. This aircraft was similar to the Boeing 707, and some observers noted that it could well be a straightforward reverse-engineered Boeing 707. Other observers suggested that it was not and that although it looked similar in the wing design, the Y-10 was quite different from the 707. Notwithstanding that debate, only two of the aircraft were built. The aircraft were heavy and uneconomical, so the program was canceled in 1983.

After this setback, the government decided on a more incremental strategy, known as the three-step plan, to enter the civil aircraft industry. Step one would be local production of foreign designs. The next step would be local development but with some overseas assistance for the development of the aircraft. The final step would be wholly independent aircraft design and manufacturing.

This strategy was started in the mid-1980s with a Shanghai facility assembling kits of the McDonnell Douglas MD-82 jet aircraft (a 150-seater aircraft). At the time, McDonnell Douglas was in the final throes of its exit from the industry and was looking for ways to radically change its business model. The idea of putting work into China was one of the driving factors for strategy at the time.

After 30 aircraft were assembled from kits in China, the plan was to move production to the later-technology MD-90 aircraft, which was the latest version of the MD80 series, but Boeing had merged with McDonnell Douglas, and the MD-90 program was canceled.

In the late 1990s, there was another foray into the civil aircraft industry by China. This was an attempt to form a consortium of Airbus, Singapore Technologies, and the Chinese aircraft manufacturing company called Aviation Industry Corporation of China (AVIC). They were going to produce a smaller aircraft, called the Air Express 100 (AE-100). This program terminated in 1999 with Airbus pulling out because of potential conflicts with its own A320 product line.

China's current effort to build an indigenous aircraft was started in the early 2000s.[10] China perceived a need for a regional aircraft of 70–100 seats and thought that a better way to enter the civil aircraft industry was with a smaller aircraft. This aircraft became known as the ARJ21 (short for Advanced Regional Jet for the 21st Century) and has just entered service with a Chinese airline, Chengdu Airlines, as this book is being written.

A lot of the ARJ21 design heritage looks like it may be drawn from the MD-80 and the MD-90, particularly with the nose, some parts of the fuselage, and the tail looking very similar to the McDonnell Douglas products.

In an approach similar to that used by the Russian Superjet program, many of the aircraft's subsystems are from Western suppliers. The engines come from GE, the avionics from Rockwell Collins, the flight control systems from Honeywell, and landing gear from Leibherr of Germany.

The program has had a long and checkered development. One of the major issues was the testing of the wing, which failed before specifications said it should. This required a major redesign and delayed the certification program.

At the onset of this program, there was an intent for the aircraft to be sold outside of China, and the program did pick up orders from Myanmar and Laos, both close allies of China. To make these orders feasible and to serve countries beyond Myanmar and Laos, it was crucial that the ARJ21 have FAA certification. At the time of writing, this looks increasingly unlikely. The aircraft has received domestic CAAC certification but has failed to receive FAA certification, and there are reports that such certification is now far into the future. The export orders for the ARJ21 from Myanmar and Laos have been canceled. Both cancellations have been rumored to be a result of the FAA certification not being forthcoming.

It is perhaps worth noting here that many of the Chinese aircraft manu-facturers have an ownership stake in the airlines in China. For example, in 2009, the Commercial Aircraft Corporation of China (COMAC) took a 76% shareholding in Chengdu Airlines. AVIC has a 26% stake in

COMAC. Soon after COMAC invested in Chengdu, the airline announced an order for 30 ARJ20 aircraft. Ultimately, the ownership (and control) of the airline can be traced back to the Chinese government.

I have a few observations on the Chinese attempt at entry into the civil aircraft industry. First, there appears to be a perception that the ARJ21 is a domestic demand-driven program. At the time of launch, there was the presumption announced by the government that there was going to be a large demand for regional aircraft in China. Such demand has not occurred, however. The airline industry in China still demands large aircraft, 150 seats and above. Aircraft demand has not migrated down to the regional class (50–100-seaters) yet, so the market for the ARJ21 has not materialized.

The other issue about the aircraft is that, because of delays in its certification, it is now becoming increasingly uncompetitive with aircraft from Bombardier and Embraer, which have upgraded their aircraft. The ARJ21 may also now be uncompetitive against the Mitsubishi MRJ of Japan. By being slow to market, the ARJ21 is thus now at risk of being leapfrogged by competitors.

An interesting development in recent years is that China's aircraft industry has been consolidated to be more national-champion-oriented than it was before. The industry was fragmented in the 1970s and 1980s, similar to Russia's, with separate design houses and manufacturing facilities. The civil side is now consolidated into COMAC, which has been designated as China's national champion for civil aircraft manufacturing. This is a good thing for the prospect of being successful in bringing an aircraft to market.

China has followed a long path of bringing a civil jet aircraft to the global market. It has almost achieved market entry with the ARJ21, but because FAA certification has eluded the aircraft, sales to the global market are not feasible. COMAC is now turning to its next new program, the C919 150-seater aircraft. COMAC has learned a lot from the ARJ21 and perhaps the C919 will be China's first FAA-certified civil jet aircraft.

Signals of Success for Aspirants

In this chapter, we explored the nascent civil jet aircraft industries of Japan, Russia, and China. We have learned for the most part that these programs appear to be going through difficulties although they may still be success-ful. Obviously, it is early yet, but both the Russian and Chinese prospects are looking rather bleak, and the Japanese prospect with the MRJ may well be overtaken by a new aircraft from Embraer.

What can we learn from the attempts by these three countries? What works and what does not work? What is the role of government? Is in-country demand important, for instance? It is it important to have a tech-nological edge? Is management of CoPS really that important? Are the overarching geopolitical issues an overriding consideration?

In Chapter 11, we will draw all these themes together into a framework that will enable us to review each country. This will help us to make judg-ments about the track record of the incumbents and how they entered, and then contrast that experience with the current attempts at entry.

11.

A Framework for Assessing Industry-Entry Success

In this penultimate chapter, I will bring together the themes explored in this book that address barriers to entering the civil jet aircraft industry. I will assess the incumbents and aspirant nations within a framework, with the aim of comparing those nations that have successfully entered with countries that aspire to enter the industry. Table 11.1 captures this assessment.

To perform this assessment, we need a set of criteria to consider the likelihood of successful market entry by an aspirant country. I will make a judgment on the relative importance of these criteria. I will then compare each country against these criteria and multiply each country's criteria rating by the importance weighting. Table 11.1 captures all this numerically. For each country, these weighted criteria scores are added to provide a total rating. This total rating is used to compare each country's civil jet aircraft industrial strength and therefore provides a way to judge how a new entrant's position compares with the positions of those who have entered the industry successfully.

Before I do this, let us remind ourselves what I mean by "market entry." The definition that I put forward in Chapter 1 involves entry into the civil jet aircraft manufacturing industry on a global scale and over the long term. For example, the Japanese YS-11 does not meet this definition. Although the aircraft was a technical success, it was a turboprop and had no follow-on product. Embraer's entry with the ERJ 145 was a success because the ERJ 145 was a regional jet, the jet sold globally, and the Brazilian company has produced follow-on aircraft.

Assessment of a country's strength in civil jet aircraft manufacturing

Type of criteria	Criteria	Importance	National criteria score 10= Fully 1 = None						
			US	EU	Canada	Brazil	Japan	Russia	China
Geopolitical	Access to current technology Western suppliers	10	10	10	10	10	10	5	6
	Certified to FAA/EASA standard	9	10	10	10	10	10	9	6
Country specific	Industrial policy stance - National champion vs tech diffusion	7	5	8	9	10	6	7	7
	Near to technological barrier	7	10	9	9	9	7	6	5
	Aerospace is a strategic industry	7	9	9	10	9	7	10	10
	Defense sector with global aspirations	5	10	6	2	3	5	9	9
	Partnering Strategy Paradox	4	10	10	10	10	5	10	10
	Ability to garner indigenous demand	3	8	8	7	7	10	7	10
	Size of home market	3	10	10	3	4	4	6	10
Product specific	Aircraft is globally competitive	7	10	10	10	10	7	7	6
	Global service network	4	10	10	10	10	6	5	3
	Second aircraft is being planned	2	10	10	10	10	1	7	7
	Total ratings ->		632	626	596	604	492	499	481

Source: Author

Table 11.1. Assessment of a Country's Strength in Civil Jet Aircraft Manufacturing

Assessment Criteria

Overall, there are 12 criteria to be considered in assessing each country's likelihood of successful market entry. These criteria are grouped into three classifications: geopolitical, country-specific, and product-specific.

- Geopolitical criteria are barriers to entry that operate at a very high global level. Most countries with important civil aircraft markets are governed by the rules and regulations of the West, which include the United States, Europe, Japan, and many other countries. To participate in the global industry, a new entrant has to abide by these rules. This criterion therefore aims to assess how a country's strategy conforms to the norms of the West.

- Country-specific criteria are many. These cover the nature of the government's intent, as well as its policies and capability to support its home civil aircraft industry.

- Product-specific criteria relate to the product itself. Here I consider the specification of the aircraft and whether it is capable of competing on a global scale. Whether the aircraft is tailored solely for the home market or the technology embodied in the aircraft is dated are typical considerations.

Geopolitical Criteria

I consider two geopolitical criteria. First is the idea of whether the country has unfettered access to current Western aircraft technology. This is important because with civil aircraft, one nation does not hold all the best technologies; it is difficult to collect and collate them together in one nation. What tends to happens is that some countries are good at one thing while other countries are good at others.

If a new entrant wants to produce a competitive product, it will need to have access to Western suppliers to produce a globally competitive product. The problem with this is that to have access to Western suppliers, the entrant comes under the jurisdiction of the US and European regulations on the transfer of high technology. In the United States, this is codified by the International Traffic in Arms Regulations (ITAR), which control the transfer of technology over national borders.

The other geopolitical constraint is whether the aircraft will be certified to Western rules—i.e., whether it has Federal Aviation Administration (FAA) or European Aviation Safety Agency (EASA) certification compliance. This could be seen as a product constraint, but the reality from a new entrant's perspective is that these rules are controlled by the West. The manufacturer has to produce a product that satisfies Western certification requirements.

Country-specific Criteria

There are many country-specific criteria. The first is the industrial policy stance of the nation. What is meant here is whether the nation is adopting a policy of creating a national champion or is more focused on technology diffusion within the country. The latter suggests that many companies in the nation will be involved in a program. The Japanese YS-11 is an example of a technology-diffusion policy, while Brazil's Embraer epitomizes the national-champion stance. National industrial policy is an important criterion and a good indicator of success.

Another criterion to consider is whether the nation overall is near the civil aircraft technological barrier. If it has a lot of technology that is close to that of the incumbents, market entry is easier. If the country is lagging in technology and buys parts and assembles an aircraft with little indigenous activity, it probably is not going to produce a competitive aircraft.

The involvement of government, as we have seen throughout this book, is universal in the civil aircraft industry. If the government of an aspirant sees civil aircraft as a strategic industry, this is beneficial to the aspirant. Canada, for example, is explicit in saying that its aerospace industry is strategic, the rationale being that the industry creates high-paying jobs, brings good technology diffusion, and enables the country to produce high-technology goods.

The role of the defense industry and its connection to the civil aircraft industry was discussed earlier in this book. This is an important connection because some technology is common on both sides of the industry. If a country has a large domestic defense industry, that is helpful (but not essential) to entry in the civil sector. The large scale of the US defense industry is advantageous to the civil business, for example.

We addressed the idea of the partnering strategy paradox in Chapter 8. Although the paradox operates at the company level it makes sense here to consider it as a country criterion since there is usually only one aspirant per nation. With this criterion, we consider the reality that as a new entrant gets closer to an incumbent company, the technological barriers to the aspirant's entry are reduced but the commercial barriers increase, given that contracts with incumbents may constrain aspirants.

A much-discussed criterion in this book is the importance of the size of the domestic industry of the new-entrant manufacturer. This can be important but is not always. It is advantageous for the new entrant to have a government that directs the aircraft to be bought by the indigenous airlines, but this demand is often not enough to close a business case for an aircraft, which requires a large amount of financial investment. That investment usually has to be recovered from a global market rather than a domestic market. Even a large domestic market like China's may not be large enough to provide an adequate financial rate of return.

In a prior chapter we discussed a particular internal tension within a nation: Advocates wanting priority focused on economic development for the whole nation, versus advocates who want to target a specific industry. The economic-development lobby is likely to desire efficient Western products, whereas the industrial-policy enthusiasts will want support for an indigenous aircraft.

The importance of securing indigenous demand from local airlines has not been demonstrated in reality. Again, Canada comes to mind, and, to a lesser extent, Brazil. Canada has a small civil market when compared to other nations, and so does Brazil, but they still successfully entered the civil jet aircraft industry.

Given the foregoing, I have split the importance of the domestic market into two criteria. One is the ability of the government to direct demand from local airline customers to the indigenous aircraft manufacturer; the other assesses the sheer size of the home market—the larger the better—but is assigned a low weighting because of the Canadian and Brazilian track records.

Product-Specific Criteria

I have three criteria under this heading. First is the global competitiveness of the aircraft. This is an important criterion because many nations considering market entry are doing it for domestic reasons. Many nations aspire to produce aircraft driven by domestic politics and perceived domestic need. Their rationales are to develop localized transportation systems at a lower cost and to reduce the cost of importing expensive Western aircraft from incumbents. The approach of tailoring the aircraft for the domestic market is not good one if the country aspires to produce an aircraft that is globally competitive. This is not a good omen for the production of a competitive civil aircraft industry for the long term.

The second product-specific criterion is the extent of planning for an aircraft service network. Much consideration of entry barriers often fails to address the fact that aircraft need servicing. Aircraft need highly skilled repair-and-overhaul individuals to maintain the aircraft to keep them flying and safe. If a company aspires to operate on a global scale, it simply must have a global service network. Such a network takes time to deploy. For many aircraft customers, a concern is how their aircraft are going to be serviced, and by whom. The track record of service delivery is an important criterion for customers to consider when making an aircraft-purchase decision.

Finally in the list of product-related criteria is if the new entrant is considering a second aircraft type. This is quite important. If an airline is buying an aircraft, it needs to be convinced that its supplier is in the business for the long term, so a manufacturer planning for a second aircraft type is a good sign. Buyers expect to fly their aircraft for twenty years or more, and they expect the aircraft manufacturer to put forward a plan to show that it will be around for that long, so if a new entrant launches an aircraft and is already painting a picture of a second aircraft to the marketplace, it is a good indicator of commitment to the market.

Assessing the Criteria for Each Country

I have numerically captured my judgments about the above criteria in Table 11.1 after assessing the evidence produced in the foregoing chapters and tapping into my own professional experience in the industry, observing the successes and failures of market entry. Clearly, these judgements are subjective.

First, I ranked the criteria in importance. For instance, the most important consideration is if an entrant wants to produce a globally competitive aircraft and if it has ready access to Western suppliers' current offerings. The new entrant will need such access for competitive participation. There are other important elements to entry, but these are not as critical. For instance, the size of a home market is important but is not always related to the success of market entry.

The criteria are ranked in the Importance column of Table 11.1; a rating of 10 is of highest importance, and a rating of 1 would be not important at all.

The other input into the framework is the rating of the particular criterion for each country. If a country has a rating of 10, it fully meets the criterion. If the rating is a low number, the country is lacking in that criterion.

Given that brief explanation of my process for populating Table 11.1 with data, let us now move on to reviewing the assessments for each country.

The United States

Clearly, the United States is a highly capable nation with a long history in the civil aircraft industry, so it is a little unfair to compare the country with new entrants, but we have to start somewhere. This nation has all the technical capabilities to participate. It sets many of the rules for participation in a geopolitical sense, and in both country-specific and product-specific criteria, the United States has strong positions.

An area that the United States is weak on is industrial policy. It is ambivalent to either targeting a national champion or supporting technology diffusion—but this is irrelevant. The US industry has consolidated to one large civil jet aircraft manufacturer (Boeing), which is now the country's de facto national champion. Despite this, in the table, I have given the country a low rating with regard to a national champion because the US government does not treat Boeing as a national champion by giving the company preferential financing or corralling domestic market demand.

European Union

Airbus can be seen as the EU national champion. In fact, Airbus was a creation of governments to compete against US companies. That desire to compete against the United States is less of a driving dynamic today, than when Airbus was created more than forty years ago, however. That is why the rating is not a 10 in the industrial policy box for the EU, though it is still a high score.

The next consideration is the scale of the EU defense industry. Each country still tends to be national in orientation, which leads to the creation of cross-border joint ventures to garner economic production volumes. Furthermore, compared to the United States, the EU defense industry is small. There is some technology crossover, but it is not as significant as we see in the United States' case. This is why I assign the European Union a moderate numeric rating of 6 for the defense sector criterion.

Canada

Going back to the national policy criterion, the Canadian government has a strong inclination to support Bombardier. This is also the case for the company's home province of Quebec, which is very supportive of the company. That is why I give Canada a high score for this criterion.

On defense market size, the rating for Canada is low. The defense industry is small, and most of the country's defense hardware is brought in from the United States or Europe.

Another area where Canada rates low is the size of the home market for civil aircraft. It would be unsustainable for Canada to rely on domestic aircraft demand to close a financial business case for developing a new aircraft.

Brazil

Brazil's industrial policy stance has been that Embraer is the national champion. The company was supported in its early days and is now an inspiring success story for the country. Similar to Airbus, the importance of Embraer being a national champion is less today than when it was in the formative stages; nevertheless, I give it the highest rating because Embraer and the Brazilian government are aligned.

Similar to Canada, Brazil has a small defense industry. It is a large nation physically, but the defense requirements are small. This does not provide much of an economies-of-scale benefit for a civil aircraft industry or a broad technology transfer route. The same goes for the size of the home market for civil aircraft; it is relatively small.

Incumbent Nation Summary

When we consider these four countries/regions—the United States, the European Union, Canada, and Brazil—and multiply the weightings with all the criteria, we have total numeric scores. The scores for these countries, the incumbents, are all coincidently just below 600 points. These four are very capable nations with self-sustaining production of world-competitive civil aircraft, and any nation that aspires to enter the civil aircraft manufacturing industry needs to be competitive against them.

I will now go on to look at the three aspirant nations, which are Japan, Russia, and China.

Japan

Japan had an attempt at entry in the 1970s with the YS-11 turboprop aircraft. Although a technological success, the attempt was not followed up by another aircraft type. Instead, the industry changed strategy and became sophisticated subcontractor to the incumbents, most notably Boeing.

Today, however, Mitsubishi is bringing to market the Mitsubishi Regional Jet aircraft (MRJ) and is using Western-supplied equipment (particularly the engines and avionics). Furthermore, the aircraft will be certified to FAA or EASA regulations. These are promising signals of a successful market entry.

A potential weakness in Japan's entry attempt, however, is the size of the domestic airline and defense markets. Another weak area is that there are no plans for a second aircraft as of the writing of this book. This is unusual because it signals to the marketplace a lack of long-term commitment to the market.

Another important consideration about the Japanese industry is that it has major relationships with incumbents. This gives rise to the partnering strategy paradox; the entrant has partnered with incumbents, so if it introduces a product that competes against one of the incumbents, there may be consequences.

Russia

In a geopolitical context, Russia needs the notional agreement of the United States and Europe to sell into their markets. In the present situation, with an impasse over Ukraine and sanctions imposed, it is difficult to see how the Sukhoi Superjet will be a great success in the Western world.

Obviously, it is too early to say, but the Superjet program is close to seeing its early success slipping away. This is not because the aircraft was particularly bad in terms of performance but because in its current form, the geopolitical environment is too adverse. This is the Achilles' heel of the program.

The other area where Russia is weak is its position on the technological hierarchy. Historically, the country has been at the leading edge of aerospace technology, but it has been a long time since dissolution of the Soviet Union and the consequent collapse of the aircraft industry when not many aircraft were developed. A lot of its aerospace skill set has therefore become dated, which is why I marked them down on that capability in Table 11.1.

The other area where I have marked Russia down is the industrial policy stance. Although much of the aircraft industry has been consolidated into United Aircraft Company, that does not mean that there are not competing agendas about priorities.

One of the strengths of Russia is that the government sees aerospace as a strategic industry. It has done so since the nation was formed, even though its transition from the USSR to Russia. Russia still has aspirations for global positioning. To achieve this aspiration, it requires an indigenous aerospace industry that is not reliant on the West. This creates a contradiction, however, because the Sukhoi Superjet 100 is very much reliant on Western suppliers.

Now that the political and geopolitical scene has retrenched, there is pressure on the domestic civil aircraft industry to source parts from within Russia. This means that any aircraft that is produced from that strategy will be weak in a global sense. Nevertheless, aerospace is seen as important in Russia, and that has a positive impetus for the development of a civil aircraft industry.

Another area of potential weakness is the development of a service network. The Sukhoi Superjet 100 was developing a network just before the Ukraine situation unfolded. Further deployment is likely to be on hold.

Of the three aspirant nations, Russia was first to market. Although it brought an aircraft to market that was reasonably competitive, particularly at highly discounted prices, its progress is currently stalled because of geopolitical considerations.

China

Of the three aspirant nations, China is currently the weakest entrant but has the strongest long-term prospects. There are several reasons for this. One is that with the ARJ21, the nation is reliant on Western suppliers, which is required to be in the global civil aircraft industry; however, this requirement exposes China to risk if there are geopolitical issues (as we have seen with Russia and the Superjet).

The bigger risk for China, however, is that it currently struggles to produce an aircraft that is certifiable by the FAA. There are questions about whether the ARJ21 will achieve full FAA certification. If it does not, China will not be able to sell it to countries that recognize FAA or EASA regulations, and that is most of the world. That is a negative for the Chinese industry.

Another aspect China as an entrant is that of the three countries considered, it is probably the weakest technologically and the aircraft is therefore heavily reliant on Western-produced parts. Because of International Traffic in Arms Regulations ITAR regulations, much of the Western parts that have been put into this aircraft tend to be a generation behind what is competitive today in Western aircraft. The West's stance to ensure that China does not use current Western technology in its defense aircraft, which means that any technology that goes into China for civil aircraft is not the latest generation. This is a negative for China, hence its low ranking for this criterion.

Another weakness for the Chinese is the need for a global service network. There is little evidence to suggest that such a network is being deployed for the ARJ21. This gives the impression that China is not really thinking about selling this aircraft on a global scale.

On the strengths side, there is evidence that the Chinese government can direct domestic airlines to buy home-produced aircraft. It seems that through government edict, the government can facilitate aircraft orders. This influence is aided by the ownership structure of some Chinese airlines. Of course, the size of the home market is large and second only to the United States in terms of scale. This again is a considerable benefit for China.

Aspirant Nation Summary

Unfortunately, from Table 11.1, we see that the three aspirants of Japan, Russia, and China all rate just below 500. It is difficult to conclude whether that level is adequate for us to conclude that they will produce a viable long-term civil aircraft industries at the moment, I believe a score above 500 would suggest a strong new entrant. Any score less than 450 suggests that an aspirant has some way to go to become a credible competitor. Of course, many things could happen yet. We will not know until five to ten years from now whether the activities from these three nations have been successful.

Chapter Summary

In this chapter, I shared a framework that subjectively assesses a nation's strategy to create a civil jet aircraft industry that can sell on a global scale. Although it is subjective, the assessment is based on opinion formed by industry experience. The framework is an empirical model of the factors for successful entry into civil aircraft manufacturing. After we have gone through the assessment process, however, it is still unclear whether the current aspirant nations will be successful. There are early indications that Russia may not be successful on a global scale because of geopolitical issues, and China's current inability to certify the ARJ21 to FAA standards is worrisome, while Japan has yet to deliver the MRJ to an airline customer. It is early days yet, however, and the results will play out over the next few years.

Let us move on to the final chapter of this book. There, I will draw some of the lessons from this examination of entry barriers in the civil jet aircraft industry. I will also look at the implications for the industry, consider some lessons on high-technology globalization and the role of government, and provide pointers to further research activity.

12.

Conclusions

The last successful entrant into the civil jet aircraft industry was Embraer, twenty years ago. It joined Airbus, Boeing, and Bombardier as the sole participants in a $6 trillion global business over the next twenty years. Why so few participants and why have we not seen a more recent entry? I think it is safe to conclude that entering the civil aircraft industry is hard—but why?

This will sound rather esoteric, but most people's conception of the world follows a linear mind model: Nations will progress through the three stages of industry in a stepwise fashion. Agriculture is followed by manufacturing, which in turn is followed by a shift to a service economy. In the same way, what a country manufactures progresses along a continuum from simple products to sophisticated products.

What we have learned, however, is that these progressions are not linear. Development is often nonlinear and happens in fits and starts. Indeed, a shift backward may occur as a result of a technological breakthrough in another country or a profound geopolitical event changing market access.

A country can quickly progress its industry along a technological advancement by adopting a strategy of following industry leaders in other countries, but the challenge then comes in transitioning from a follower to a leader, operating at the technological frontier. Civil aircraft are products at the technological frontier.

Another area of misconception is the role of government in high-technology industries. The narrative of the brilliant inventor creating a new industry on his or her own is not accurate. Much more prevalent is that government takes an active role in facilitating innovation, and this innovation would not take place without government. There are numerous examples of this, such as Thomas Edison's electrical power revolution, the Apple iPhone, and Google's search engine. All these technological milestones were achieved with engagement of government in their early development.

Government is involved with civil aircraft manufacturing for a multitude of reasons. This includes correcting the financial market's failure to invest in high technology, and stimulating technology diffusion and job protection, so when evaluating the factors affecting entry into the aircraft industry, a consideration of a government's role is vital. This is why it is a major subject considered in this book.

Airbus, Boeing, Bombardier, and Embraer produce remarkable machines. Aircraft have their own life-support systems to enable passengers to survive traveling five miles above the Earth's surface at speeds of 500 miles per hour. At any given time over the United States, 5,000 civil aircraft carrying nearly half a million people are estimated to be aloft. Is it any wonder that many emerging countries want to enter this exciting industry? Their intents are to create a new industry, facilitate knowledge diffusion, lower the cost of acquiring aircraft for domestic use, and demonstrate their own technological prowess.

In this book, we have looked at how the four incumbent aircraft manufacturers entered the industry. This was used to guide an assessment of the success of Japan, Russia, and China's attempts at entry, which was a tough judgment call. Russia has brought an aircraft to market, but its success is constrained by the fallout of geopolitical developments. China's recent aircraft has not received FAA certification yet, and we await Japan's entry into service in 2018. It is too early to tell whether these countries will be successful.

The trials and tribulations of the current new entrants has not diminished the enthusiasm of other nations to enter into civil aircraft manufacturing. The list of countries includes India, Indonesia, Mexico, Morocco, and South Korea. Although they all participate as suppliers to the incumbents, several have advocates suggesting that they should become independent manufacturers and follow the example of Embraer. The framework defined in this book may help to inform them in assessing their ambition's feasibility and to indicate the best developmental strategy to make it happen. Finally, the framework described here could be applied with modifications to other civil aerospace sectors such as business jets and small general aviation aircraft.

But remember, entering the civil aircraft industry is hard!

Glossary

airframer	a company that designs and manufactures aircraft
aerostructure	a component of an aircraft's airframe that typically includes the fuselage or wings
AMP	Advanced Manufacturing Partnership, an activity launched by the US president in 2011
ARJ21	Advanced Regional Jet for the 21st Century (China)
avionics	electronic equipment fitted in an aircraft
BEA	British European Airways
BNDES	Banco Nacional de Desenvolvimento Econômico e Social (Brazil)
BOAC	British Overseas Airways Corporation
CEO	chief executive officer
COMAC	Commercial Aircraft Corporation of China, Ltd
comparative advantage	the ability of a country to produce goods at a lower opportunity cost than other countries
CoPS	complex product systems
CTA	Command for Aerospace Technology (Brazil)

DARPA	Defense Advanced Research Projects Agency
DASA	Deutsche Aerospace AG (Germany)
DOD	Department of Defense (US)
EADS	European Aeronautic Defence and Space Company
EASA	European Aviation Safety Authority
Embraer	Empresa Brasileira de Aeronáutica (Brazil)
EU	European Union
FAA	Federal Aviation Authority (US)
GDP	gross domestic product
GDP per capita	a measure of the average wealth per person within a nation
GE	General Electric
geopolitics	a term for describing global rivalries in world politics
IPR	intellectual property rights
IT	information technology
ITA	Instituto Tecnológico de Aeronáutica (Brazil)
market failure	occurs when the allocation of goods, services, and capital is not efficient
MBB	Messerschmitt-Bölkow-Blohm (Germany)

MITI	Ministry of International Trade and Industry (Japan)
MRJ	Mitsubishi Regional Jet (Japan)
NAMC	Nihon Aircraft Manufacturing Company (Japan)
NASA	National Aeronautics and Space Administration
NATO	North Atlantic Treaty Organization
OECD	Organisation for Economic Co-operation and Development
oligopoly	a market that is shared by a small number of companies
partnering strategy paradox	a paradox that arises because as a company acquires more technical skills from a partner, it becomes more commercially linked to that partner
power plant	the engine, along with other components, that provide the power source for an aircraft
R&D	research and development
Snecma	Société nationale d'études et de construction de moteurs d'aviation (France)
strategic trade theory	a government policy to affect the outcome of competition in an industry dominated by a small number of firms
technology diffusion	the process by which innovations are adopted by a country and population as a whole

three-sector model	an economic theory that divides country economies into three sectors of activity: extraction of raw materials (primary), manufacturing (secondary), and services (tertiary)
TRL	technology readiness level
turbofan	a jet engine in which a turbine-driven fan provides additional thrust
turboprop	a jet engine in which a turbine is used to drive a propeller, or an aircraft powered by a turboprop
UK	United Kingdom
US	United States
USSR	Union of Soviet Socialist Republics (also known as Soviet Union)
WTO	World Trade Organization

Endnotes

Chapter 2

1. See Acemoglu (2012), Berger (2013), Holzer (2011), Joffe (2014), Liveris (2011), Smil (2013).
2. Clark was a British and Australian economist and statistician, and Fourastié was a French economist.
3. I used data from the Central Intelligence Agency's 2011 Fact Book, GDP(PPP) in US$
4. For example: Cheng (2015) and Fishman (2012)
5. For example: Andersen (2001)
6. Helper (2012)
7. Jensen (2011)
8. Bain (1956), but also see Geroski (1991) and Yip (1982)
9. Jacobides (1997)
10. Mueller and Tilton (1969)
11. For example: Begg (1997), Reekie (1987), and Hay (1979)

Chapter 3

1. Freeberg (2014)
2. Brooke (2013)
3. Geisst (2000)
4. I am reminded of a well-known quote from Frank Whittle one of the creators of the jet engine "The invention was nothing. The achievement was making the thing work"
5. Norman and Verganti (2014)
6. See Twiss (1990), Tidd and Bessant (2009), and Narayanan and O'Connor (2010).
7. Nelson (1993), Lundvall (1995), Stoneman (1995), and Dodgson and Rothwell(1994)
8. Mazzucato (2013)
9. Block (2008)
10. For example, the Federal-Aid Highway Act of 1956 was enacted by President Eisenhower.
11. Krugman and Smith (1994), but also see Brander and Spencer (1985) and Busch (2001).

12. Mazzucato (2013)

Chapter 4
1. Segal (2011).
2. Lin (2012)
3. Joffe (2014)
4. See the seminal paper on CoPS (Hobday, 1998) broadened in Davies and Hobday (2005).
5. Weiner (1990)
6. Vincenti (1990). Also see the lighter treatment in Madhaven (2015)
7. Friedman (2005)
8. It is a real benefit to my course at the University of Virginia to have Jeff as a guest speaker. He is very well qualified in the area of export control.

Chapter 5
1. Hartley (2014). For historical perspectives, also see Bright (1978) and Stekler (1965).
2. Gunstone (2009)
3. Pickler and Milberry (1995), MacDonald (2002)
4. Hotson (1987)
5. Rodengen (2009)
6. Hayward (1994, p. 33)
7. Pattillo (1998)
8. For more information, see the excellent Cliff (2011) and Fallows (2012).
9. Perrett (2013)
10. Antara (2015)
11. *Financial Express* (2014)
12. Hurriyet Daily News (2015)
13. ProMexico (2011)
14. Eriksson (2013)
15. Garvin (1998)
16. Connors (2010)
17. Sullivan and Milberry (1989)

Chapter 6
1. Bain (1956)
2. Reuters (2011)
3. Wright (1936)

Chapter 7
1. For example: in Stoneman (1995)
2. Moran (1994)
3. In 2014, the Research, Development, Test and Evaluation (RDT&E) expenditure for the US Air Force was $23.8 billion. Much of this was for advanced aircraft.
4. Staniland (2003, page 138). Staniland quotes BOAC UK House of Commons Select Committee Report HC Deb 22 July 1964, vol. 699, cc. 491–623.
5. For various views, see Newhouse (2007), Pandey (2010), and Kemp (2006).
6. Goldstein, (2002)
7. Government of Canada (2005)
8. Dolbec (2015)
9. Sullivan and Milberry (1989)
10. Pinelli (1997)
11. Fallows (2012), Cliff (2011)

Chapter 8
1. A fascinating insight into this subject can be found in Chapter 14 of Brian Rowe's 2005 memoir, in which he describes many examples of politics and the engineer.
2. *Flight International* (1994; 31 January, 28 February, 20 June 1995; 7 March, 11 June, 3 September, 26 September, 24 October 1996; 25 February, 30 April, 25 February, 25 March, 22 July 1997), *Aviation Week and Space Technology* (1997), *Aerospace Daily* (1996), *Les Echos* (29 May, 30 May 1996), Reuters (1997)

Chapter 9
1. Hooker (1984)
2. Golich (1997), Bright (1978)
3. Boeing (2016), ASME (1994)

4. According to Cook (1991, p. 214), some of the cost of the Dash-80 prototype could be charged to the government via independent R&D. This is an allowance the US government allows to be charged to compensate for R&D spent by companies that is not covered directly in cost-plus contracts.

5. Bright (1978, pp. 89–90)

6. Sutter and Spencer (2006)

7. Tang, 2009

8. Staniland (2003)

9. Gunstone (2009)

10. Phip (2007)

11. For the UK government aspect, see Hayward (1983, p. 20). For the story from a personality and technological viewpoint, see Dempster (1958) and Verhovek (2010).

12. Pickler and Milberry (1995)

13. Avro came very close to beating the Comet to being the first manufacturer of a civil jet aircraft, with the C102, flying the prototype within days of the Comet's first flight. Continued delays on a military program led to a stoppage of work on the aircraft in 1951, however, and it was then eventually cancelled.

14. Hadekel (2004)

15. Dolbec (2015)

16. Rodengen (2009), Goldstein (2002)

Chapter 10

1. Samuels (1994). An Ne-20 is on display at the Steven F. Udvar-Hazy Center, an air and space museum in Chantilly, Virginia.

2. Samuels (1994)

3. Samuels (1994)

4. Kimura (2007)

5. Committee on Japan (1994)

6. *Moscow Times* (2014)

7. Associated Press (2016)

8. Crane (2014), Goldstein (2005), Bitzinger (2012), Eriksson (2010), Sweeney (2008)

9. Fallows (2012)

10. Cliff (2011)

Bibliography

Aboulafia, R. (2014, November). Embraer backgrounder. *www.richard-aboulafia.com/shownote.asp?id=423*.

Acemoglu, D. R. (2012). *Why nations fail: The origins of power, prosperity, and poverty.* New York: Crown Publishing Group.

AMP Steering Committee Report. (2012). *Report to the president on capturing domestic competitve advantage in advanced manufacturing.* Washington, DC: Executive Office of the President.

Andersen, P. (2001). *Competitive assessment of the US large civil aircraft aerostructures industry.* Washington, DC: US International Trade Commission.

Andersen, P. (2010). *China emergent military aerospace and commercial aviation capabilities.* Washington, DC: Security Review Commission.

Antara. (2015, July 30). R80 aircraft prototype to be manufactured by 2016. *LKBN ANTARA.*

ASME. (1994, September 24). The Boeing 367-80, Jet transport prototype mechanical systems. *American Society of Mechanical Engineers.* https://www.asme.org/getmedia/5fb07cd6-0e20-41e2-87c7-4543849b98ae/178-Boeing-367-80.aspx

Associated Press. (2016, June 8). Russia looks to revive its aircraft industry with new plane.

Bain, J. (1956). *Barriers to new competition.* Cambridge, MA: Harvard University Press.

Begg, D. F. (1997). *Economics.* Maidenhead, England: McGraw-Hill.

Berger, S. (2013). *Making in America: From innovation to market.* Cambridge, MA: MIT Press.

Bitzinger, R. (2012, January 18). China and commercial aircraft production: Harder than it looks. *China Brief*, The Jamestown Foundation, Vol. XIII, Issue 2.

Block, F. (2008). Swimming against the current: The rise of a hidden developmental state in the United States. *Politics and Society 36, no 2 (June) 169-206.*

Boeing. (2016). Boeing Model 367-80. *http://www.boeing.com/history/products/model-367-80..*

Brander, J. & Spencer, B. (1985). Export subsidies and international share rivalry. *Journal of International Economics*, Vol. 18, pp. 83–100.

Bright, C. (1978). *The jet makers: The aerospace industry from 1945 to 1972.* KS: Regents Press of Kansas.

Brooke, B. (2013, March 21). Many minds produced the light that illuminated America. *US News.*

Brzezinski, Z. (1997). *The grand chessboard: American primacy and its geostrategic imperatives.* New York: Basic Books.

Busch, M. (2001). *Trade warriors: States, firms, and strategic-trade policy in high-technology competition.* Cambridge, England: Cambridge University Press.

Central Intelligence Agency (2011), Fact book - https://www.cia.gov/library/publications/download/download-2011/

Cheng, A. (2015, May 1). Record number of manufacturing jobs returning to America. *MarketWatch*, p 3.

Cliff, R. O. (2011). *Ready for takeoff: China's advancing aerospace industry.* Santa Monica: RAND Corporation.

Committee on Japan. (1994). *High-stakes aviation: US–Japan technology linkages in transport aircraft.* Washington, DC: National Academy Press.

Connors, J. (2010). *The engines of Pratt & Whitney: A technical history*. Reston, VA, US: American Institute of Aeronautics and Astronautics.

Cook, W. (1991). *The road to the 707: The inside story of designing the 707*. Bellevue, WA, US: TYC Publishing.

Crane, K. L. (2014). *The effectiveness of China's industrial policies in commercial aviation manufacturing*. Washington, DC: RAND Corporation.

Davies, A. & Hobday, M. (2005). *The business of projects: Managing innovation in complex prodcuts and systems*. Cambridge, England: Cambridge University Press.

Dempster, D. (1958). *The tale of the Comet*. New York: David McKay Company, Inc.

Demsetz, H. (1973). Industry structure, market rivalry, and public policy. *Journal of Law & Economics*, Vol. 16. No 1, pp 1-9

Dodgson, M. & Rothwell, R. (1994). *The handbook of industrial innovation*. Cheltenham, England: Edward Elgar Publishing.

Dolbec, M. (2015, June 15). Quebec ready to back Bombardier. *National Post*.

Eriksson, S. (2010). China's aircraft industry: Collaboration and technology transfer—the case of Airbus. *Journal of Technology Transfer and Commercialization*, Vol. 9, Issue 4. pp 306-325

Eriksson, S. (2013). The aircraft industry as a tool for economic and industrial development—The case of Indonesia. In E. Eriksson (ed.), *Clusters and Economic Growth in Asia* (p. 141-164). Edward Elgar Publishing.

Fallows, J. (2012). *China airborne*. New York: Pantheon Books.

Ferguson, P. & Ferguson, G. (1994). *Industrial economics: Issues and perspectives*. London: The Macmillan Press, Ltd.

Financial Express. (2014, April 16). India puts civil aircraft plan back on runway. *Financial Express.*

Fishman, C. (2012, December). The Insourcing Boom. *The Atlantic,* www.theatlantic.com/magazine/archive/2012/12/the-insourcing-boom/309166/.

Freeberg, E. (2014). *The age of Edison: Electric light and the invention of modern America.* Penguin, New York.

Freeman, C. (1995). The "National System of Innovation" in historical perspective. *Cambridge Journal of Economics,* Vol. 19, no 1, pp. 5–24.

Frenkel, O. (1984). Flying high: A case study of Japanese industrial policy. *Journal of Policy Analysis and Managment,* Vol 3. Issue 3, pp. 406–420.

Friedman, T. (2005). *The world is flat: A brief history of the twenty-first century.* New York: Farrar, Straus and Giroux.

Garvin, R. (1998). *Starting something big: The commercial emergence of GE aircraft engines.* Reston, VA, US : American Institute of Aeronautics and Astronautics.

Geisst, C. (2000). *Monopolies in America: Empire builders & their enemies from Jay Gould to Bill Gates.* New York: Oxford University Press.

Geroski, P. (1991). *Market dynamics and entry.* Oxford, England: Basil Blackwell.

Goldstein, A. (2002, August). Embraer: From national champion to global player. *CEPAL Review* 77, pp. 97-115.

Goldstein, A. (2005). *The political economy of industrial policy in China: The case of aircraft manufacturing.* The William Davidson Institute.

Golich, V. P. (1997). The evolution of large commercial aircraft in the US—An overview. In T. B. Pinelli (ed.), *Knowledge diffusion in the US Aerospace Industry* (p. 1). Greenwich, England: Ablex Publishing Corp.

Government of Canada. (2005). *National aerospace and defence strategic framework*. Ottawa: Industry Canada.

Gunstone, B. (2009). *Airbus: The complete story*. Yeovil, England: Haynes Publishing.

Hadekel, P. (2004). *Silient partners: Taxpayers and the bankrolling of Bombardier*. Toronto, Canada: Key Porter Books.

Hartley, K. (2014). *The political economy of aerospace industries: A key driver of growth and international competitivness?* MA: Edward Elgar Publishing.

Hay, D. M. (1979). *Industrial economics: Theory and practice*. Oxford, England: Oxford University Press.

Hayward, K. (1983). *Government and British civil aerospace: A case study in post-war technology policy*. London, Manchester University Press.

Hayward, K. (1994). *The world aerospace industy: collaboration and competition*. London: Gerald Duckworth & Co.

Helper, S. K. (2012). *Why does manufacturing matter? Which manufacturing matters? A policy framework*. Washington, DC: Brookings.

Hobday, M. (1998). Product complexity, innovation and industrial organisation. *Research Policy*, Vol. 26 no 6, pp. 689–710.

Holzer, H. L. (2011). *Where are all the good jobs going? What national and local job quality and dynamics mean for US workers*. New York: Russell Sage Foundation.

Hooker, S. (1984). *Not much of an engineer*. Shrewsberry, England: Airlife Publishing.

Hotson, F. (1987). *The De Havilland Canada Story*. Toronto, Canada: CANAV Books.

Hurriyet Daily News. (2015, September 17). Emerging Turkish jet to create up to 4,000 jobs. *Hurriyet News*.

Jacobides, M. (1997). Technology, firm attributes and industry structure: Assessing the dynamics of success in innovation. *Managing in the Global Economy VII, 7th International Conference*. Dublin: Eastern Academy of Management.

Jensen, J. B. (2011). *Global trade in services: Fear, facts and offshoring*. Washington, DC: Peterson Institue for International Economics.

Joffe, J. (2014). *The myth of America's decline: Politics, economics, and half a century of false prophecies*. New York: Liveright Publishing.

Kemp, K. (2006). *Flight of the Titans: Boeing, Airbus and the battle for the future of air travel*. London: Virgin Books Ltd.

Kimura, S. (2007). *The challenges of late industrialization: The global economy and the Japanese commercial aircraft industry*. Basingstoke, England: Palgrave MacMillan.

Krugman, P. & Smith, A. (1994). *Empirical studies of strategic trade policy*. Chicago: University of Chicago Press.

Lin, J. (2012). *The quest for prosperity: How developing economies can take off*. Princeton, NJ: Princeton University Press.

Liveris, A. N. (2011). *Make it in America*. Hoboken, NJ: John Wiley & Son.

Lundvall, A.-B. (1995). *National systems of innovation: Towards a theory of innovation and iterative learning*. London: Pinter.

MacDonald, L. (2002). *The Bombardier story: Planes trains and snowmobiles*. Etobicoke, Canada: John Wiley & Sons.

Madhaven, G. (2015). *Think like an engineer: Inside the minds that are changing our lives*. London: Oneworld Publications.

Mazzucato, M. (2013). *The entrepreneurial state: Debunking public vs. private sector myths*. New York: Anthem Press.

McGuire, S. (2007). The United States, Japan and the aerospace industry: From capture to competitor. *The Pacific Review*, Vol 29, Issue 3, pp. 329–350.

Moran, T. M. (1994). Aerospace and national security in an era of globalization. In D. Mowery (ed.), *Science and technology policy in interdependent economies* (pp. 173–198). Norwell: Kluwer Academic Publishers.

Moscow Times. (2014, August 28). What plane will Russia fly if Boeing and Airbus ditched over sanctions. *The Moscow Times.*

Mueller, D. & Tilton, J. (1969). Research and development costs as a barrier to entry. *Canadian Journal of Economics*, Vol II, Issue 4.

Narayanan, V. & O'Connor, G. (2010). *Encyclopedia of technology & innovation managment.* Chichester, England: John Wiley & Sons, Ltd.

Nelson, R. (1993). *National innovation systems: A comparative analysis.* Oxford, England: Oxford University Press.

Newhouse, J. (1983). *The sporty game.* New York: Alfred A Knopf.

Newhouse, J. (2007). *Boeing versus Airbus: The inside story of the greatest international competition in business.* New York: Alfred A Knopf.

Norman, D. & Verganti, R. (2014). Incremental and radical innovation: Design research versus technology and meaning change. *Design Issues*, Vol. 30, Issue 1, pp. 78–96.

OECD. (2010). *Measuring innovation: A new perspective.* Paris: OECD Publications.

Pandey, M. (2010). *How Boeing defied the Airbus challenge.* Pandey, M.

Pattillo, D. (1998). *A history in the making: 80 turbulent years in the American general aviation industry.* New York: McGraw-Hill.

Perrett, B. (2013, November 4). South Korea continues to probe turboprop despite collapse of Bombardier negotiations. *Aviation Daily.*

Phip, M. (2007). *The Brabazon Committee and British Airliners 1945–1960.* Stroud, England: Tempus Publishing.

Pickler, R. & Milberry, L. (1995). *Canadair, the first 50 years.* Toronto, Canada: CANAV Books.

Pinelli, T. B. (1997). Japanese technological innovation—Implications for large commercial aircraft and knowledge diffusion. In T. B. Pinelli (ed.), *Knowledge diffusion in the US aerospace industry—Part B* (p. 829-889). Greenwich, England: Ablex Publishing Corp.

Pritchard, D. & MacPhearson, A. (2008). *The emergence of Japan as a subsidized competitor in the commercial aircraft sector: The new trade war.* Canada-United States Trade Center.

ProMexico. (2011). *Mexico's aerospace industry road map 2011.* ProMexico.

Reekie, W. C. (1987). *Managerial economics.* Oxford, England: Allen.

Reuters. (2011, July 19). Rolls-Royce, Pratt & Whitney settle patent battle. *Reuters.*

Roberts, D. & Singh, R. (1997). The Japanese civil aero-engine industry: Will it challenge the Western hegemony ? *Managing in the Global Economy VII, Proceeding of the 7th International Conference* (p. 66). Dublin: Eastern Academy of Managment.

Roberts, D. (2013, January). Aftersales service—Part of the purchase package. *Professional Pilot.*

Rodengen, J. (2009). *The history of Embraer.* Fort Lauderdale, FL: Write Stuff Enterprises, Inc.

Rowe, B. &. (2005). *The power to fly: An engineer's life.* Reston: American Institute of Aeronautics and Astronautics.

Samuels, R. (1994). *Rich nation strong army: National security and the technological transformation of Japan.* Ithaca, NY: Cornell University.

Segal, A. (2011). *Advantage: How American innovation can overcome the Asian challenge.* New York: Norton & Co, Inc.

Singh, R. (1996). Fifty years of civil aero gas turbines. *Fiftieth Anniversary Lecture, 5th June 1996,* Cranfield University.

Smil, V. (2013). *Made in the USA: The rise and retreat of American manufacturing*. Cambridge, MA: MIT Press.

Staniland, M. (2003). *Government birds: Air transport and the state in Western Europe*. Oxford, England: Rowman & Littlefield Publishers.

Stekler, H. (1965). *The structure and performance of the aerospace industry*. Los Angeles: University of California Press.

Stoneman, P. (1995). *Handbook of the economics of innovation and technological change*. Oxford, England: Basil Blackwell Ltd.

Sullivan, K. & Milberry, L. (1989). *Power: The Pratt & Whitney Canada story*. Toronto, Canada: CANAV Books.

Sutter, J. & Spencer, J. (2006). *747: Creating the world's first jumbo jet and other adventures from a life in aviation*. New York: HarperCollins Publishers.

Sweeney, P. (2008). Flying without succeeding? Assessing the future of the China aviation manufacturing sector in the People's Republic of China. *Journal of International Policy Solutions*, Vol. *8*, Issue 3, pp 1-17.

Tang, C. Z. (2009). Managing new product development and supply chain risks: The Boeing 787 case. *Supply Chain Forum: An International Journal*, Vol. 10, Issue 2 pp 74-86.

Tidd, J. & Bessant, J. (2009). *Managing innovation: Integrating technological, market and organizational change*. Chichester, England: John Wiley & Sons, Ltd.

Twiss, B. (1990). *Managing technological innovation*. London: Pitman Publishing.

Verhovek, S. (2010). *Jet age: The Comet, the 707 and the race to shrink the world*. New York: Avery.

Vincenti, W. (1990). *What engineers know and how they know it: Analytical studies from aeronautical history*. London: Johns Hopkins University Press.

Weiner, E. (1990, December 19). New Boeing airliner shaped by the air-lines. *New York Times*.

Wright, T. (1936). Factors affecting the cost of airplanes. *Journal of Aeronautical Sciences*, 122.

Yip, G. (1982). *Barriers to entry: A corporate-strategy perspective*. Lexington: Lexington Books.

Index

CPSIA information can be obtained
at www.ICGtesting.com
Printed in the USA
FFOW02n2323161117
43487831-42190FF